Seeds, Embryos, and Sex

Also by Margaret Cosgrove

BONE FOR BONE
EGGS — AND WHAT HAPPENS INSIDE THEM
PLANTS IN TIME
THE STRANGE WORLD OF ANIMAL SENSES
STRANGE WORLDS UNDER A MICROSCOPE
WONDERS INSIDE YOU
WONDERS OF THE TREE WORLD
WONDERS OF YOUR SENSES
WONDERS UNDER A MICROSCOPE
YOUR HOSPITAL, A MODERN MIRACLE

SEEDS, EMBRYOS, AND SEX

Written and illustrated by
Margaret Cosgrove

DODD, MEAD & COMPANY
New York

To my niece, Margaret Lee Conrad

Copyright © 1970 by Margaret Cosgrove
All rights reserved
No part of this book may be reproduced in any form
without permission in writing from the publisher
Trade ISBN 0-396-06205-9
Dodd Durable ISBN 0-396-06221-0
Library of Congress Catalog Card Number: 79-114236
Printed in the United States of America

Contents

PART I

    1. How Plants Leave Home   7
    2. Secrets of the Seed   11
    3. Flower Power   17
    4. Journey to the Two-Sex Way   21

PART II

    5. Animals and Embryos   31
    6. The Mother   33
    7. The Father   41
    8. Why?   45

    Index   61

PART ONE

1. How Plants Leave Home

This is a story of the very beginnings of living things—of plants and animals, of you—how they get their start at the very instant when the spark of life is struck.

This is a story that goes back before that instant into the lives of parents and grandparents and even before them, to tell of how the spark of life is passed along. It is a story of children and parents—do all living things have two parents? Do any have none, or one, or three? Do they all grow in the dark world inside one parent before being born into the light of day, and for those that do, how do they get into that dark world, and come out of it?

This is a story that points out some astonishing ways that plants and animals are alike in their beginnings, and something of how the offspring have come to look like their parents. Of how both plants and animals travel in one way or another, and how the grown males and females of both pass on the spark of life and inheritance to new beings.

And we will look into the answer to the very big question of *why*. Why does the system of sex, the two-parent system, turn out to work better then the many other methods that have been used? Let's start to find out.

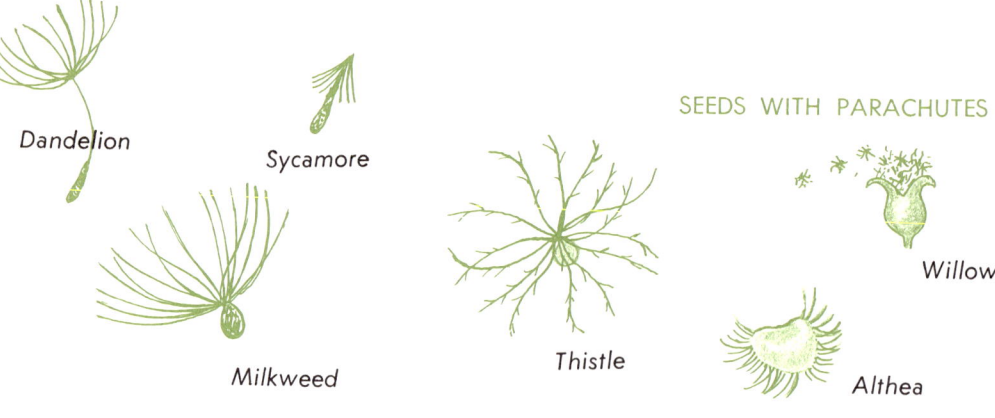

SEEDS WITH PARACHUTES

Dandelion, Sycamore, Milkweed, Thistle, Willow, Althea

   Start with a seed. You are surrounded by seeds. Almost every kind of tree, bush, and smaller flowering plant gets seeds on it sooner or later. Before we delve into the inside of some seeds themselves, and the matter of where they came from, let's look at some outsides—the containers the actual seeds are in. If you started a list right now of all the kinds you can think of and kept adding to it for the next year, you would notice something remarkable: how many kinds there are. There are tiny jewel-like seeds, and big coconuts in their huge cases. There are pits in peaches and "stones" in cherries. There are beans and peas and peanuts in pods. There are seeds in containers with fuzz or fluff attached, or little parachutes as dandelion seeds have, and with wings of all varieties, and many with prickles and hooks all over them that hitch a ride on your clothes, or on your dog's fur in autumn when you hike through woods or field. There are nuts and acorns and berries, and the grains that breakfast cereals are made from.
   Just about every kind of fruit you eat has seeds inside but there are exceptions, and bananas don't. Corn is seeds, and watermelons contain plenty of seeds to spit out—who hasn't discovered that? It's fun to watch seeds grow, though there is some skill required to sprout and raise them to become healthy plants.
   Seeds with fruit or pulp around them (such as apples, pumpkins, tomatoes) may attract birds or four-legged animals to eat them,

and the seeds often go right on through the animal undamaged, to be dropped sometimes miles away. This is one of the best ways of hitching a ride to a far-off spot.

Why are there so many kinds of seeds? If a maple tree had ten thousand seeds on it, can you imagine what would happen if they all just fell to the ground beneath it and began growing right there? Most would be healthy and off to a good start—but then what? The little trees would become as high as your ankle and start to shove, jostle, and crowd, and before they were knee-high most would probably be sickly and weak from lack of space. None from this particular tree would be growing anywhere else in the world but here, in the shade of the parent. Only two or three might ever grow into big trees, and the rest would all sooner or later die.

So seeds must travel. For most kinds it is too late to travel by themselves once they have put out a root, so they must do it before they sprout, as soon as they have left the parent tree. Maple seeds each have a wing on their container and grow as twin seeds, two wings joined together that break apart, usually, when they spin

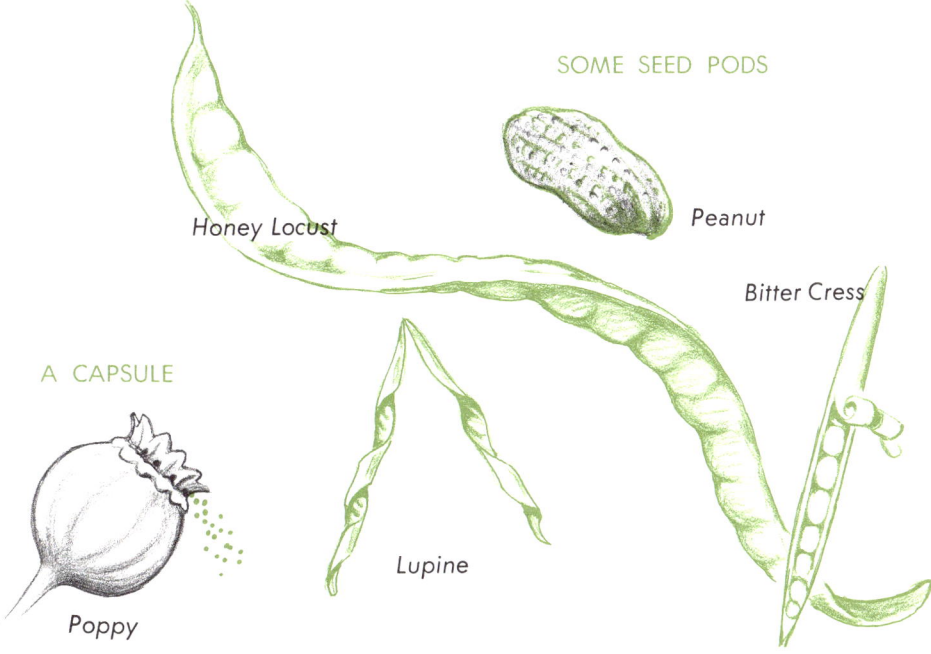

SOME SEED PODS

Honey Locust

Peanut

Bitter Cress

A CAPSULE

Lupine

Poppy

away from the tree. The wings also slow down their falling speed so the wind can catch them and whiff them a distance away.

Some kinds of seeds fly, others go for a sail on water. Some are gliders, some propellers, parachutes, or kites. There are those that hitchhike on fur or feathers, dress or pants. The whole tumbleweed plant out West breaks off at the ground and goes tumbling before the winds across the prairie miles, spilling a trail of seeds behind it. There are gluey seeds that stick to the feet of birds. There are seeds in capsules that are shaken out as though from salt shakers.

Many are the other ways. Inside the prickly, fuzzy, or winged container, the seed itself is resting before beginning active life.

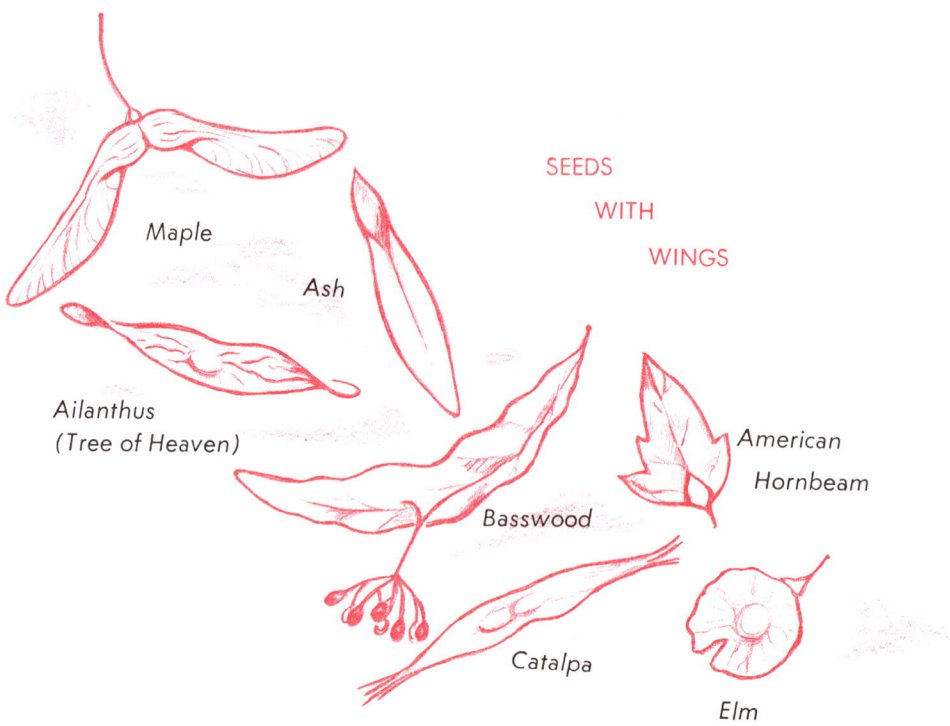

SEEDS WITH WINGS

Maple
Ash
Ailanthus (Tree of Heaven)
Basswood
American Hornbeam
Catalpa
Elm

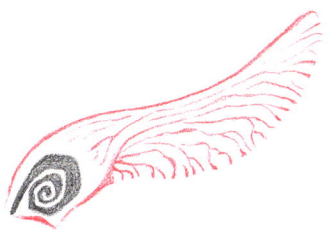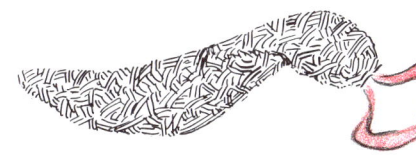

2. Secrets of the Seed

We have looked on the outsides of some seeds and noticed great diversity, which is a way of saying variety. That is, we have observed how many kinds of seed containers there can be to enable trees and smaller plants to travel, and seeds to leave home and seek their fortunes. Seeds are more alike on the inside than the outside; there are many small differences among them, but they are built on a basically similar plan.

Examining the inside of a seed is like getting close to the heart of a secret. Regardless of what the seed container looks like from the outside, or whether it is big or small, the seed itself must have the start of a whole little plant inside it. This is called the *embryo* (em-bree-o). A beginning plant, a beginning animal, before either is developed enough to live by itself, is an embryo. A kitten, puppy, or human baby, in its early stages of development before birth, is called an embryo.

Look at the next big tree you see and think about it. Did all that come out of one small seed? In a way it did. An explosion is what it was, in slow motion. If you could speed up fifty years of a tree's growth into ten seconds, you would see a fantastic explosion, but one of creation, not destruction. The fuel, the energy, the material came from the soil, sun, and rain, but every single cell of the tree itself sprang from another back all the way to the tiny embryo in the seed.

We will take a seed out of its container (for example, the seed out of a grapefruit or a bean out of its pod) and look at it. The seed

SEEDS THAT CLING

Tick Trefoil   Sandspur   Cocklebur   Beggar's Tick

itself is rather like a package with a set of equipment inside it. The embryo needs a food supply in the seed to grow on, and will need more energy during its days of sprouting. Certain things that happen to the seed unlock this kit like a key unlocks a treasure chest. Moisture and warmth are the keys, and sometimes time. Suitable soil must be in readiness, and sunshine (or at least light) for the embryo when it emerges.

The seed itself is made of:
1. Outer wrappings that contain
2. an embryo, and
3. a food supply.

The outer wrappings are waterproof and weatherproof, though they must let in a little air and moisture. The embryo itself is made of the starting parts of a root, stem, and leaves. The food supply is for the embryo to live on until it is able to obtain its own food through the roots and make it within the leaves.

You can do a three-bean experiment. Dried beans will be suitable if they are soaked a few hours first. One of these (or several) you can plant (instructions, page 13). One may be saved for Chapter 3. One can be opened carefully.

Notice the wrappings of this bean. There is a tough, outer one and an inner, very delicate one. Inside these you find that the bean is divided into two halves. Open these like a book, trying not to break them apart at first. It helps to have a magnifying glass handy for what you are about to see. At one end of the seed, between the halves, is the little embryo itself, curved and pearly white. It is complete: the root, the stem, the tiny leaves. At the tip of the root, and at a growing tip between the leaves, are the few cells that, pushing downward and upward, will produce the cells of the whole splendid, mature plant. Seeing an embryo in a seed is like discovering a pearl in an oyster, but this pearl is filled with the magic of the life force.

One bean (or several) may be planted, in a flower pot or other container, with a little layer of soil pressed over it, and watered often enough to keep the soil moist but not soaking. A window sill is a good place for the pot, if the sun is not too blazing. Soon the seed will sprout, or *germinate*. Day by day you can observe the silent, slow-motion explosion. Stem and leaves and greenness will stream upward, a beautiful sight, every cell developed from the original embryo.

Before the little root could get food from the soil, the plant was nourished by its own food supply. The bean you opened up split into halves. The planted bean came up with the two halves attached to the stem. Gradually they shriveled up and finally fell off. The stem had drawn the food out of these until the root could take over in feeding the plant. These are called seed leaves, or food leaves, or *cotyledons* (cot-ill-*lee*-dons).

Most seeds you plant will have two seed leaves. On some kinds of plants these stay in the ground, or even in the seed, as in the case of acorns (from oak trees), and do not come up looking at all like leaves. Some plants have only one seed leaf, or cotyledon. Corn is a one-seed-leaf plant or monocot (*mono* meaning "one"), but the cotyledon stays inside the seed here, too. The bean is a two-seed-

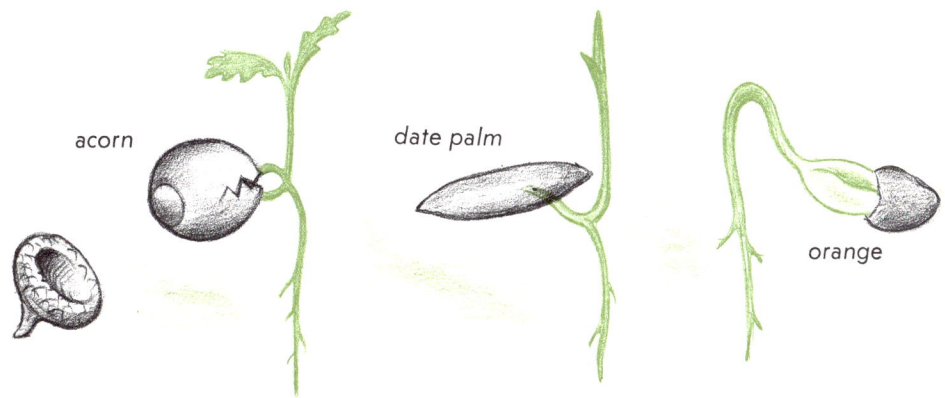

acorn

date palm

orange

leaf plant, or dicot (*die*-cot, *di* meaning "two"). A palm seed is from a monocot plant, as you will see if you plant a date seed, which takes much waiting, skill, and patience (use some sand with the soil in the potting mixture), but is worth it for the beautiful but slow-growing date palm tree you may get for your trouble. Seed leaves are a little as if you ate your lunch from a lunch box packed for you every day until you were old enough to start providing food for yourself.

Growing seeds is a never-ending experiment and you could fill up a whole notebook with your observations. What would happen if you carefully removed the seed from its wrappings and then planted it? What would happen if you cut off one seed leaf, or both, as soon as the little plant has appeared? What happens if you turn the seed upside down, with the root pointing upward, after it has germinated?

Some seeds germinate right away, others take practically forever. An orange or grapefruit seed may reward you by germinating in a week or two. But a fresh apple seed will not. Think of a basic difference between the way oranges and apples grow. Orange groves flourish in warm, mostly all-year-round sunny climates, such as Florida and California. Apple trees prefer the North, and need a cold winter season. These trees planted in the South have been unable to bear good crops of apples. It is interesting also that apple seeds need to have a resting period for a time after the apple is ripe. This period, three months of "getting ready," are the *after-ripening* period. After-ripening is needed by many seeds that grow where winters are long and cold.

Seeds, then, rest or are *dormant* (Latin, meaning "sleeping") for a short time or long. Weeds come up in fields long after they have been plowed for crops, because the weed seeds have been dormant. Willow tree seeds are no longer able to sprout after only a few days of seeking a spot to grow in the spring, but experiments have shown that seeds of ragweed (a plant whose pollen is a cause

SOME KINDS OF SEED CONTAINERS

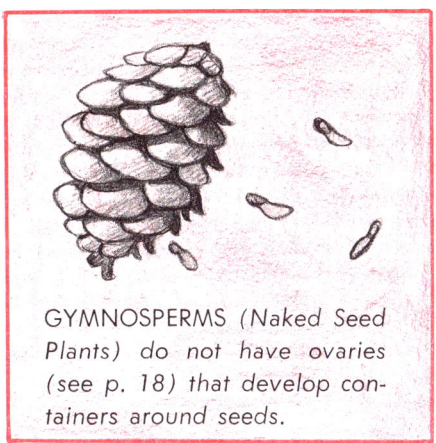

GYMNOSPERMS (Naked Seed Plants) do not have ovaries (see p. 18) that develop containers around seeds.

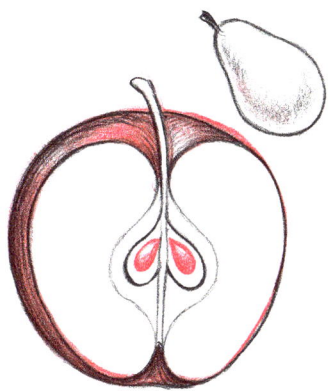

POME: Ovary forms leathery middle layer around seeds. Apple, pear

AGGREGATE FRUIT: Develops from several pistils in one flower. Raspberry

ANGIOSPERMS (Covered Seed Plants) are flowering plants and have seeds formed in ovaries that grow into containers surrounding the seeds.

TRUE BERRY: Entire ovary becomes fleshy and edible. Tomato, grape

FALSE BERRY: grows from ovary plus other parts of flower. Banana, melon

MULTIPLE FRUIT: Comes from cluster of flowers. Pineapple

of hay fever) are able to live up to forty years, and sweet clover seeds up to eighty years. But the real record may be held by lotus seeds. (Lotuses resemble water lilies.) Some of these were found frozen from ancient times in swamps in Manchuria. When they were discovered, defrosted, and planted, many actually germinated and grew to produce flowers, and were determined by scientific tests to be over a thousand years old!

There is great strength in the seed, for young seedlings have been known to force their way through tiny cracks, splitting and moving stones in their growth, or breaking through asphalt sidewalks or sun-baked earth almost as hard as concrete. In watching the slow-motion explosion, you are seeing a greater force on earth than bombs: seed power.

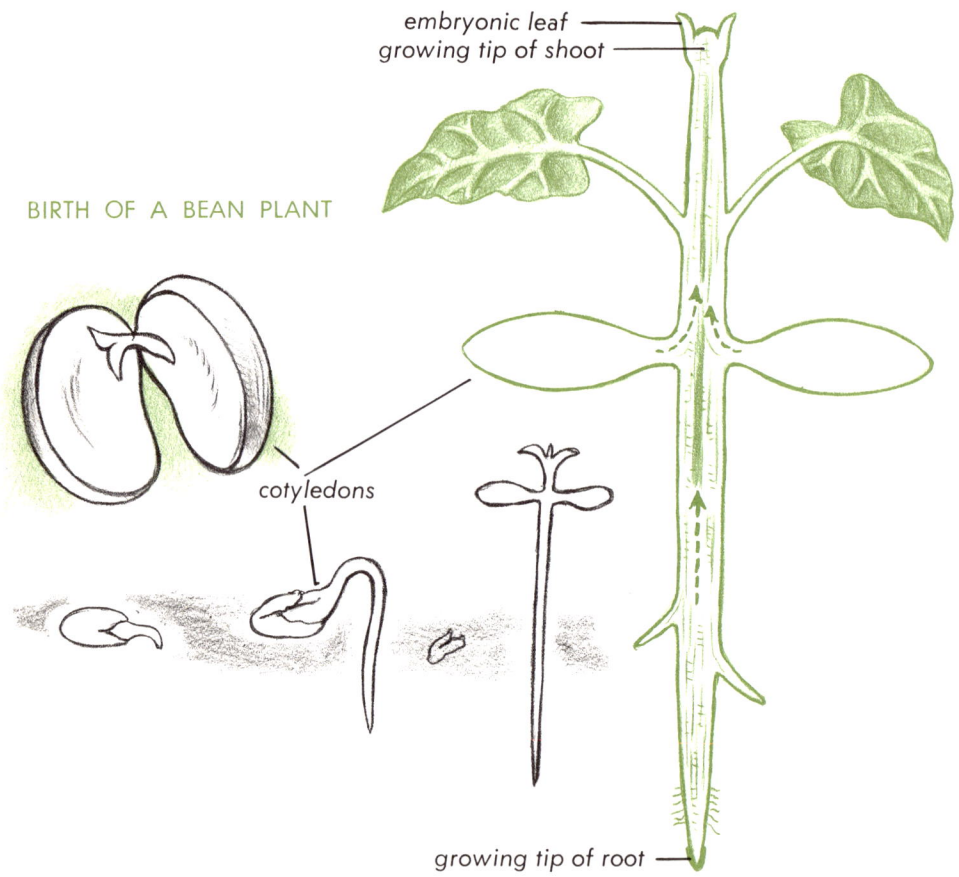

BIRTH OF A BEAN PLANT

3. Flower Power

If you could do some careful surgery on several flowers, you would notice the interesting fact that flowers, like seeds, are much alike even while they are so showily different from each other. That is, they are built on the same basic plan, but there is almost never-ending variation on the plan.

Let's take a typical flower, if there is such a thing, and work from the outside in, starting with the *sepals*. These are usually, but not always, small and green, and were the outside of the bud before the rest of the flower opened out of them. The *petals* themselves, larger and beautifully colored, often form a cup, though in some flowers (such as sweet pea), they have taken on a little different shape. You can notice in dozens of flowers the patterns of their different petals.

In the cup of petals are slender threads. Here you must look quite closely, and it helps to have a magnifying glass at hand. There is usually a ring of five or more of these threads making a circle around a center one. The outer ones are called *stamens,* and have slipper-like tops on them (*anthers*) which produce a sort of yellow powder in them. This is what you may get on your nose when you smell a lily or tulip or rose. The thread that stands in the center, different in appearance from stamens, is the *pistil*. It is crowned with an interesting top also, often fuzzy or sticky. The stamens and pistil are the most important parts of the flower.

If you trace the pistil down to its bottom and cut away the other

17

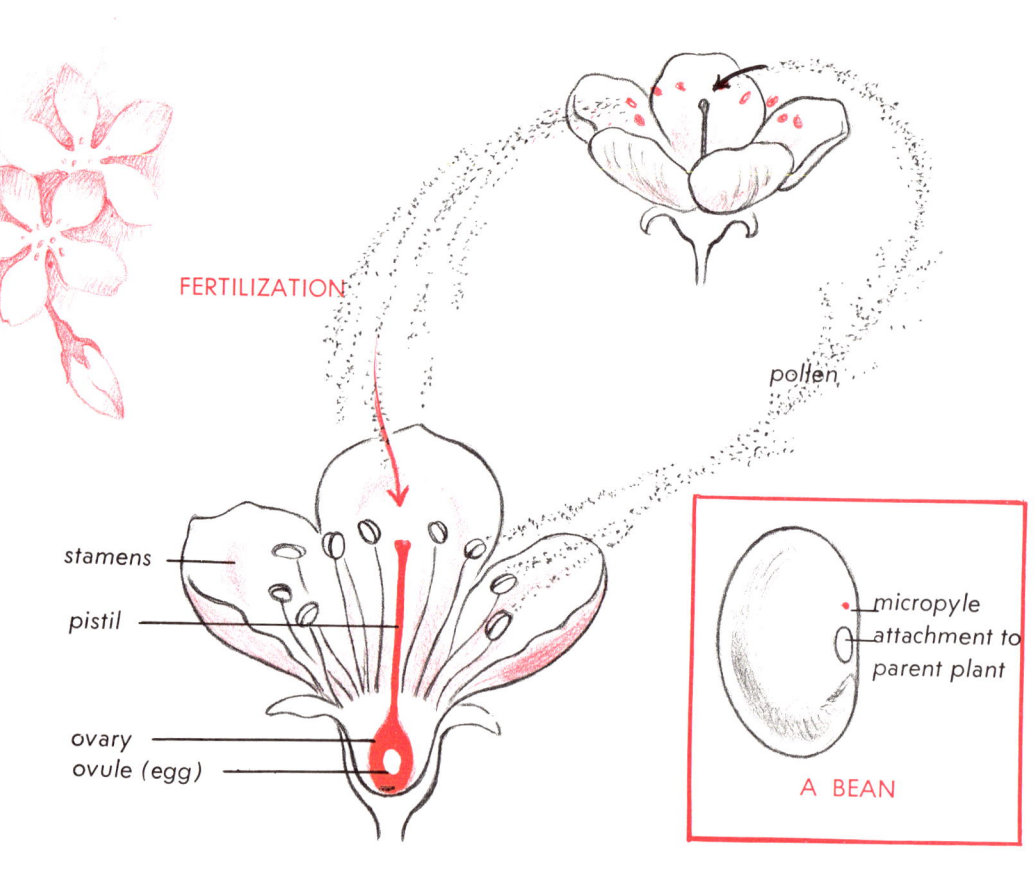

parts (petals and sepals) from one side of it, you will see how it swells out at the base. Cut this swelling open and you will see what look like tiny pearls. These are eggs. It is these that will develop into the seeds.

But not until the pollination process begins. Go back to the top of the stamens and pistil and examine them closely. The yellow powder, or *pollen,* from the stamens lands on a pistil, not usually of the same flower, and adheres to its stickiness. Out from one pollen grain grows a tiny tube that winds down through the pistil, all the way to the swelling at its base. It finds its way into the swelling, or *ovary* (meaning "place where eggs are made") and to an egg. Inside of the tip of the tube is a mere speck, the *sperm*, even smaller than the egg. The instant the sperm meets the egg the two unite, and the seed begins forming. This is the moment of fertilization. It takes a different pollen grain for each egg.

When you examine a bean, you will find several markings on one side. The largest oval shows where a stalk connected the ovary to the growing seed (now called an *ovule*, from the Latin *ovum*, meaning "egg"). A tiny hole (the *micropyle*) above this oval scar shows where the pollen tube went in to meet the egg. If you dissect this bean, you will find the root tip right beneath this hole.

The sperm has fertilized the egg, or set off its development. Fertilization is something that happens throughout most of the world of plants as well as animals. Many, or most, of all living things are either one or the other of two types: they are either male or female, and this, then, is their sex. The stamens are the male part of the flower, the pistil is the female part. Sometimes both are on one flower, sometimes on separate ones. When the male sex cell, or sperm, fertilizes the female sex cell, or egg, the embryo starts growing from the union of these two parent cells.

The pollen of one flower often fertilizes an egg of another flower of the same kind because the stamens and pistil of the same flower usually ripen at different times. The pollen's way of getting to another flower is almost always either by wind or insects.

DRUPE:

Inner wall of ovary hardens around seed to form pit or "stone." Peach, plum, olive, cherry, coconut

Flowers pollinated by wind are usually small and not at all showy, such as those of many trees and most grasses. Think of the large quantities of pollen these make, when only a few of the number are likely ever to reach other flowers in the bigness of the outdoors.

What a contrast are the insect-pollinated flowers! They are usually bright-colored, often fragrant, and with all kinds of markings, tricks, and devices that lure bees and butterflies, wasps, flies, and beetles to them. The business carried on between insects and flowers would take chapters to tell. Many of these flowers have nectaries that make a sweet, delicious fluid, or nectar. Insects, particularly honeybees, fly from flower to flower, collecting nectar and pollen for themselves and their young to eat. By accident, pollen catches on their hairs, legs, body, and mouth parts, and in this way hops a free ride to another flower. And so, what with insects, and seeds, and the fruit they bring, and their beauty, there is no end to the influence of the flower.

4. Journey to the Two-Sex Way

Anything as complicated as seeds, and the flowers and fruits they brought with them, usually were developed very, very slowly; the idea needed to be worked out over many years, and we wonder how, and how long ago, seeds began. They have only existed on earth for some millions of years, which isn't very long, as earth time goes. Before seeds, what?

First try to picture what living things must have been like, long before there were any seed-bearing plants. Around a half-billion years ago, the only plant types of life, as well as animal types, were probably very tiny ones living in the waters. There were still other kinds that could have been called either plants or animals; they seem to have been somewhere in between the two. At least these are what we feel rather certainly must have been among the first kinds of life, and we can study similar ones now, under the microscope—little plants and animals and half-and-halfs—and get a good idea of what may have lived in the early waters.

All these had to make new ones of themselves—to reproduce. The simplest way was to pinch in through the middle and break in two. You can sometimes watch this happen through the microscope and it is called *fission*. Fission means cutting or breaking into pieces—in this case, into two parts.

There is one peculiar one-cell form which no one can decide for sure whether it is plant or animal. It is called *Euglena*. It is often found in pools and country ponds. One particular kind is green in-

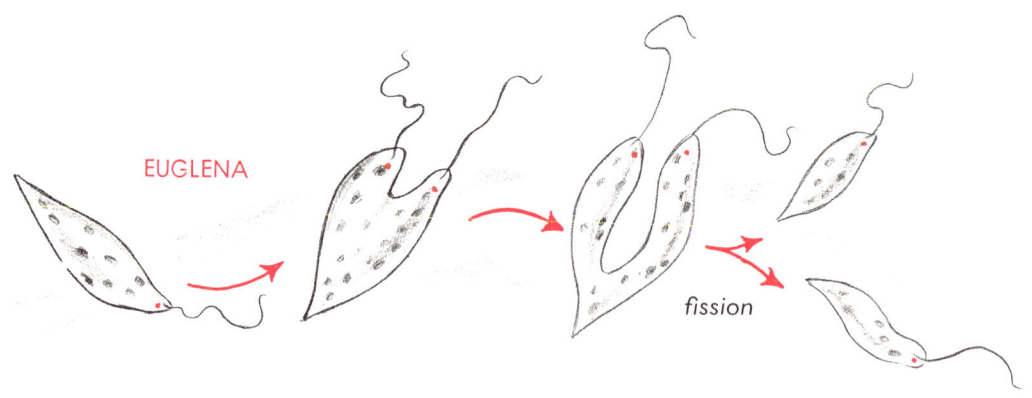
fission

side, like a plant, but swims and crawls freely, like an animal. Furthermore, it has a red dot in one end called an eye-spot. The little *Euglena* reproduces by splitting the long way into two *Euglenas*, each with a sort of whip on its front end which it lashes about, and which causes it to swim. Fission is the only known way these green *Euglenas* reproduce.

The green scums that grow in the ponds, lakes, and streams, swimming pools, and fish aquariums, are extremely interesting to study. There are many kinds of these *algae* (al-jy) in the world. They are probably quite closely related to the first plant life ever to appear on earth. Most of these fresh-water algae are bright green, but their relatives, the seaweeds are brown, red, and some are also green. There are much bigger kinds of salt-water algae than of fresh-water kinds; they are the ones you often get your feet tangled up in when they are washed up on ocean beaches.

If there was in those early times no seed in all the world, how could the algae reproduce, and how do they manage today?

There is one kind you can easily find, and this is good for examination with a microscope, if you or your school has one. When the weather is wet it may "come out" on trees; it grows on bark in humid places as a thin veil of green. Some can be raised easily at home by putting almost any twig or small branch in a glass of water (some twigs leaf out beautifully in winter), and most likely after a few days or weeks a green "scum" will collect on the bottom of the glass. This is *Protococcus*—perhaps the simplest plant that exists anywhere. Each plant is just a small dot, green as an emerald. Each one simply divides in two to reproduce—this is fission again.

The kind of algae that streams like green mermaid's hair from underwater stones or dead leaves, or floats in a cloud just beneath the surface, may be the very common but beautiful *Spirogyra*. Each long, fine strand simply starts growing again when nibbled in two by a fish, or broken by a boat or swimmer, and that is the way it reproduces. In late fall *Spirogyra* breaks up into pieces by its own accord, and each fragment begins growing again in early spring.

But there is a surprising twist in the so-far dull life of *Spirogyra*, for sometimes two strands come to lie alongside each other and little bridges grow from one to the other. Each cell has its own bridge to a cell of the other strand. The insides of one cell flow through its bridge to join with the contents of the cell on the other side, where a little ball is formed. This is a *zygospore*. The zygospores burst out of a strand, sink, and rest (usually through the winter) until the next growing season, when a new *Spirogyra* strand sprouts from each. The zygospores may look like very small seeds—but are not.

A slightly different kind of green algae with the name of *Ulothrix* has still another way of reproducing, besides its way of breaking into fragments which grow long again. It produces little green swimmers that swarm out of some cells. These are called *zoospores* (*zo*-oh-spores). Each zoospore has four short whips on the front that move it actively. Zoospores swim about for a while before settling down to grow into new *Ulothrix* strands. But *Ulothrix* uses

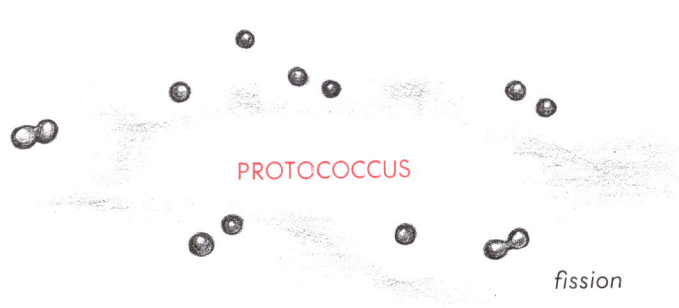

PROTOCOCCUS

fission

still another method of reproducing. It produces little two-whip green swimmers, and two of these (from different strands) come together and join into a single little ball—a zygospore. After this zygospore's resting period (usually on lake or pond bottom, during the winter), four new *Ulothrix* strands begin growing out of each—the zygospore was a kind of sexual reproduction.

Now let's go to the ocean to examine a fascinating big seaweed that grows only in salt water. Many or most of these marine algae can continue growing in sea water after they are broken in two. Rockweed, the very common brown seaweed that can often be found growing from rocks, has its own story to tell. Hollow cushions on these, like small balloons, keep them afloat. But Rockweed bears a second kind of balloon also, which are the swellings at the tips of many of the rubbery branches. A pinpoint hole can be seen on each of the tiny bumps that cover them. Inside the balloons,

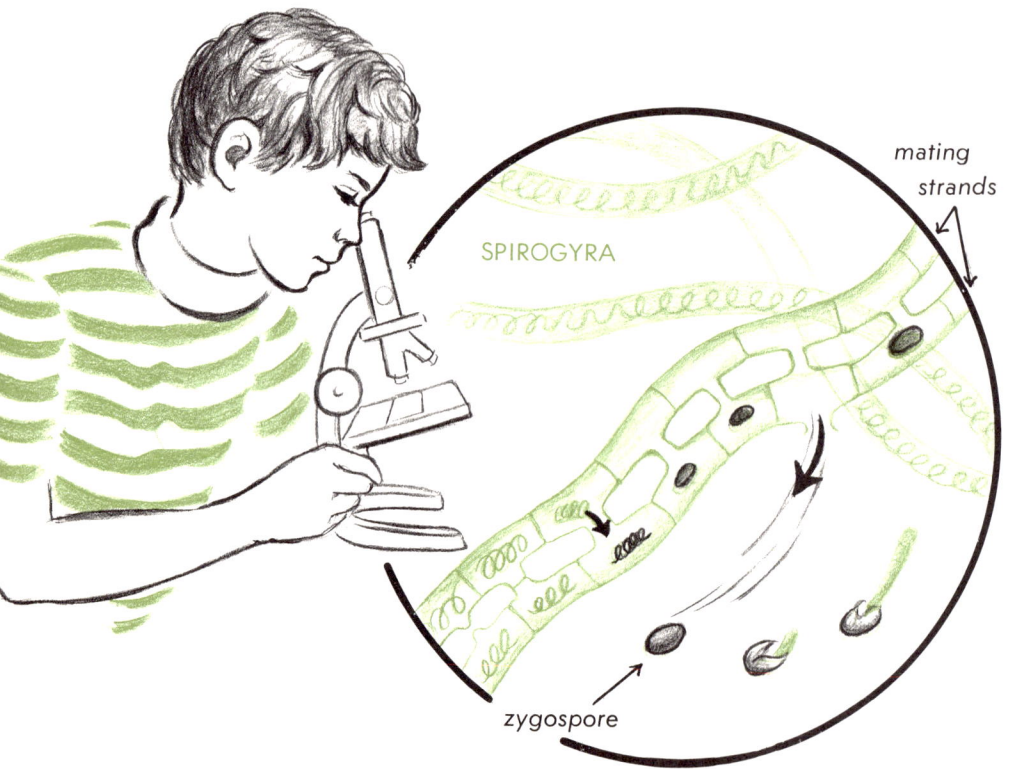

SPIROGYRA

mating strands

zygospore

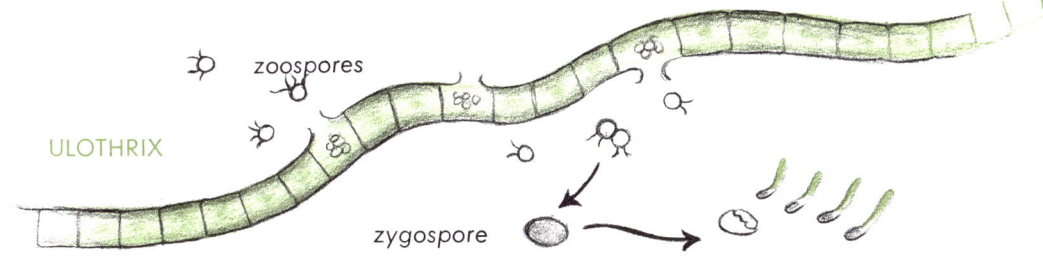

two kinds of special cells are being made. One kind is larger; they are *eggs*. The other, smaller kind, each with two whips (properly called *flagella*), are *sperms*. We have seen something that looked like sperms before; they were zoospores, but zoospores live by themselves, and sperms do not for long.

This is how it happens. It is most often at low tide, when the brown seaweed dries out for a while, that the swellings shrink and squeeze out the eggs and sperms, which often come from separate swellings but sometimes from the same one. When the tide returns, the sperms swarm around the eggs in the water, and when a sperm meets an egg a *zygote* is formed. The zygote is tossed off through the waves, and starts growing into a new Rockweed when it has found a spot of rock to attach itself to. Eggs and sperms meet, but they do not produce anything like a seed. Many are the ways of reproducing that the algae have, and all are engrossing to study.

After a very long time of life on earth there came great forests, the trees and smaller plants of which looked hardly anything like what we see on earth now (though a few small-sized samples of those do remain). But neither in these dreamlike forests nor any place else across the land was there a single flower or seed or fruit as we know them, in all the world. Land plants could not let loose a flood of zoospores to swim away, so how were they to do their reproducing? They used air-borne spores this time—dry, tiny specks as small as grains of powder. One tree could let loose a whole breezeful of millions, even billions, of spores.

But these strange, towering forests did not keep new ones coming for 50 million years as simply as by throwing out clouds of spores that grew at once into more tall trees. What the spores grew into were something that didn't look at all like the tree they came from. They became very small *gametophytes*. Sometimes these grew flat on the ground, looking like tiny leaves, sometimes down in it. If we could go back through time to stroll, big-eyed with wonder, through a Spore Forest, we would probably walk right over the gametophytes and never notice one at all.

But important things can happen in little, low places, and the gametophytes made two special kinds of cells on them, and one of these could swim through a drop of moisture to the other. These were sex cells, male and female, and two would unite, and after a time would grown into another Spore Forest tree or smaller plant. This was a sort of take-turns, or alternating, way of reproduction—the one-spore, then the two-sex-cell ways, with both methods required to produce one tree.

But somewhere, somehow, an unknown tree was finding a new way that would bring far-reaching changes to the world. It is some mystery tree that did it, for scientists are not sure exactly how this new idea began.

This unknown plant took two giant steps forward in its way of reproducing that caused an astounding occurrence: the seed. In fact, this is the first half of an exceedingly important double-happening in the story of living things.

First, it started making two kinds of spores. One was probably smaller than the other. The sperm was *inside* this one, instead of having to originate on the little gametophyte, where it could swim.

Second, the bigger spore, instead of being blown off the tree, somehow remained on it, where the smaller one came to it. An egg cell was *inside* this larger one, and when the sperm, coming out of its spore where it was kept moist, joined with an egg, it fertilized it. With the egg continuing to be held on the tree, three things were made possible:
  1. The embryo got *protection* from the parent, and
  2. it received *nutrition* from it, so that
  3. it would have all the *time* for safe growing it needed.

AN IMPORTANT HAPPENING

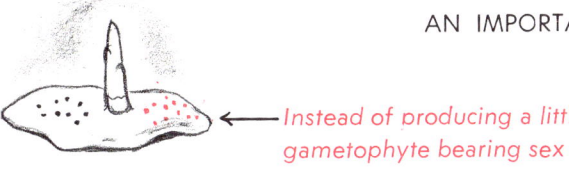

Instead of producing a little gametophyte bearing sex cells—

some plant of long ago was able to hold the female sex cells on it where they were fertilized.

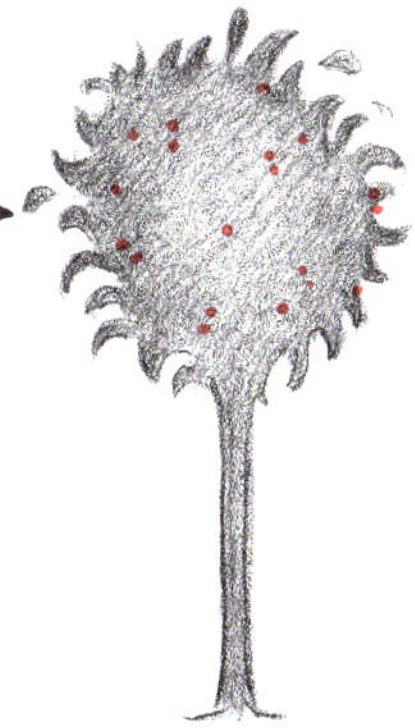

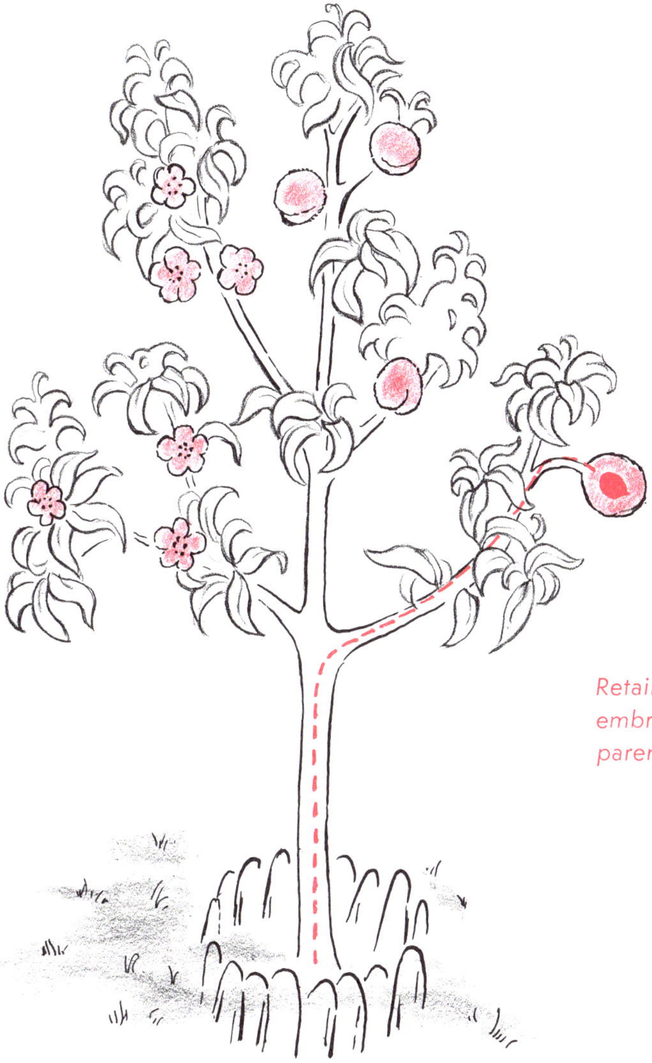

Retaining the embryo on the parent gives it
    1. Protection
    2. Nutrition
    3. Growing time

ROCKWEED

It all ties in together. The early spores from the one-spore trees were too tiny to carry food in them, so if they didn't start growing right away into the little gametophyte, they would get no nutrition; they had to be tiny so they could be blown; they had to be tiny because there were so many; there had to be many because only a few might land on a good growing place; because they were so tiny they could never carry a whole embryo inside them.

The great occurrence, the seed, also brought some astonishing new excitement into the world. Wind blew the pollen, in many cases. But somehow another kind of explosion began. Riots of petals bloomed around stamens and pistils, and brought color to the drab earth, and the flower brought fragrance and sweet nectar —and buzzing across the woods and meadows. For insects coming into being were attracted by the sights and smells and tastes, and plants and insect life flourished because each needed the other for survival. You have only to sit quietly on a summer's day and watch a flower, or a clump of flowers, for an hour, to see its little visitors

MOSS

Spores can be found in the capsules.

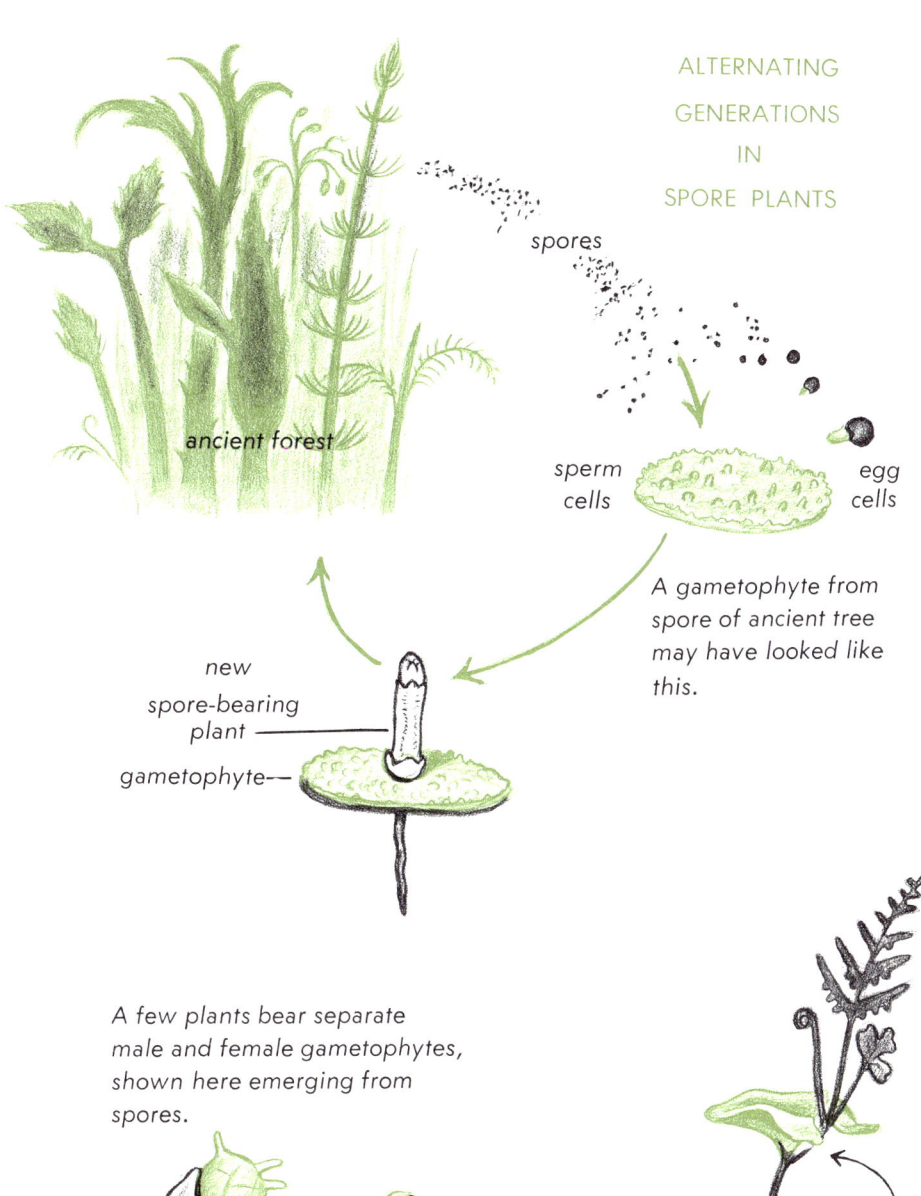

ALTERNATING GENERATIONS IN SPORE PLANTS

ancient forest

spores

sperm cells

egg cells

A gametophyte from spore of ancient tree may have looked like this.

new spore-bearing plant

gametophyte

A few plants bear separate male and female gametophytes, shown here emerging from spores.

♀

♂

Gametophyte of present-day fern.

♀ = female
♂ = male

flashing and fluttering and crawling, to imagine the emptiness of a world without the flower, the seed, the fruit.

The small ovary grows enormously to become the seed container, which is the pod, nut, or prickle-ball around the seed. It is the ovary walls that become the fruit of the peach or cherry or watermelon, with its rind. Sometimes the ovary grows wings on it, or sails or fluff, to speed the seed on its travels.

We have seen two basic kinds of reproduction. Sometimes one individual, like the *Euglena* or *Spirogyra*, split in two, or broke into many fragments, or put out zoospores that grew: one made many. Or the opposite: two plants or special cells came together to make one zygospore, or an embryo in a seed. The seed way, with a long time to develop on the parent, was so successful that it took over most of the earth from the Spore Forests, and brought the beauty of flowers and the noise and busyness of insects and a magnificent wealth of new food and life and pleasure with it.

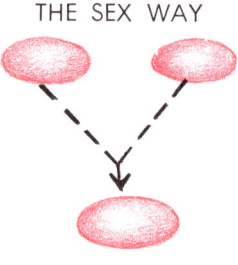

THE NON-SEX WAY

one makes two

(or many)

THE SEX WAY

two make one

(except in some cases of multiple births such as identical twins, where one fertilized egg divides into two or more individuals).

PART TWO

5. Animals and Embryos

We have seen how plants, including even the tallest trees, start out as very little embryos. Animals also grow from embryos, from a single cell. A great many animal embryos develop in eggs—butterflies and spiders, snakes and turtles, frogs and birds, for example. But human beings and almost all furry, four-legged animals do not come from eggs. They develop inside the mother until they are born.

Whether embryos grow in the egg or in the mother, they have similar needs, and these are for protection from hardship and weather, nutrition, and time to grow. The shell gives protection, and most egg-laying mothers take care to deposit their eggs in a location most favorable to their offspring. Inside the new-laid egg is an almost invisibly small embryo and a rather enormous food supply. The two exchange places and sizes as the embryo grows by using up the food supply. (You can see this in a hen's egg: the food is the yolk, or yellow part. The embryo also makes use of the

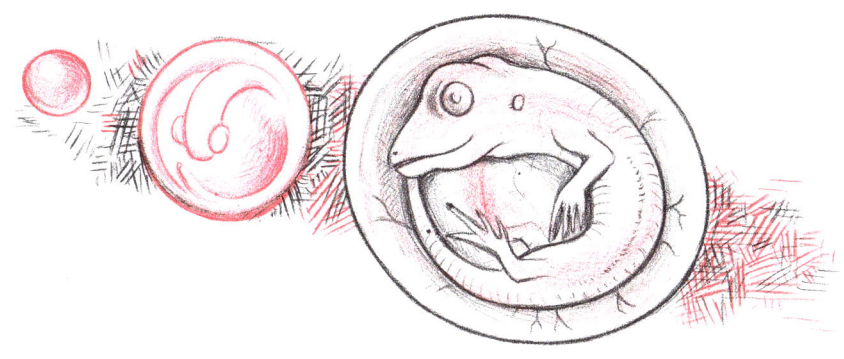

white part.) It is something of a miracle the way the young creature will grow into an almost exact copy of its parents. All the food, water, and protection it needs it will find in its closed, private world.

The period of being formed inside the egg or its mother's body is the most important time of any animal's entire life. Every embryo, by the time of hatching or birth, will have already made every part it will ever have—at least the starting cells for each part. The puppy, kitten, or human embryo grows in its mother's *womb* (pronounced "woom"), and we will take an imaginary look into that dark place and time. But first we must find out what we will be looking at.

We will be looking at mammals. These are the four-legged animals with fur or hair, almost all of them not hatched from eggs, but born from the mother, after the period of development, inside her. Animals hatched from eggs do almost all their developing after the egg has left the mother. There is another way that makes mammals different from animals hatched from eggs. The mothers of all mammals can feed their young by nursing them with milk made by glands in their bodies. The human mother has two breasts which fill with milk around the time her baby is born. The furry mother may have several pairs of teats (for example, the cat has four or five pairs) through which the young are suckled. The cow or goat has udders. And mammals give the longest period of care of any animals to their offspring, preparing them to look after themselves.

6. The Mother

Mammals stay inside their mothers to develop for different lengths of time. It takes a mouse three weeks, a lion about three and a half months, a bear about six months, a camel about one and a half years. The chimpanzee, cow, and human being each take about nine months.

Let's look at a kitten in its mother's womb, or uterus (*you*-ter-us). There are probably several more embryos there with it. Each one is in a separate sac, or "bag of waters," in which the animal floats. This protects it as the mother jumps and runs and lies down. The kitten begins as a tiny cell, about the size of a dot you would make with a very sharp pencil. This cell itself, called an *ovum*, was made in the mother's ovary inside her body. The ovum came down a tube to the uterus. Here in the uterus the ovum united with a sperm from the father cat and was fertilized, and started its development. The round egg cell divided into many cells and became a very small, hollow ball which soon began to lengthen a bit, changing constantly, until it looked slightly like a fish. Its brain, its eyes, and other organs began to appear, and after a while its heart had taken form and began to beat. At first it gave just an occasional pulsation but slowly the beating became more regular. Its limbs, when they began, looked merely like lumps, but in a few weeks the embryo was looking like a true little mammal. Soon it began to squirm about. After about two months in the uterus it had a little fur, and was ready to be born. (Cats and dogs have a period of development in the womb of from sixty-three to sixty-six days.) As it and its

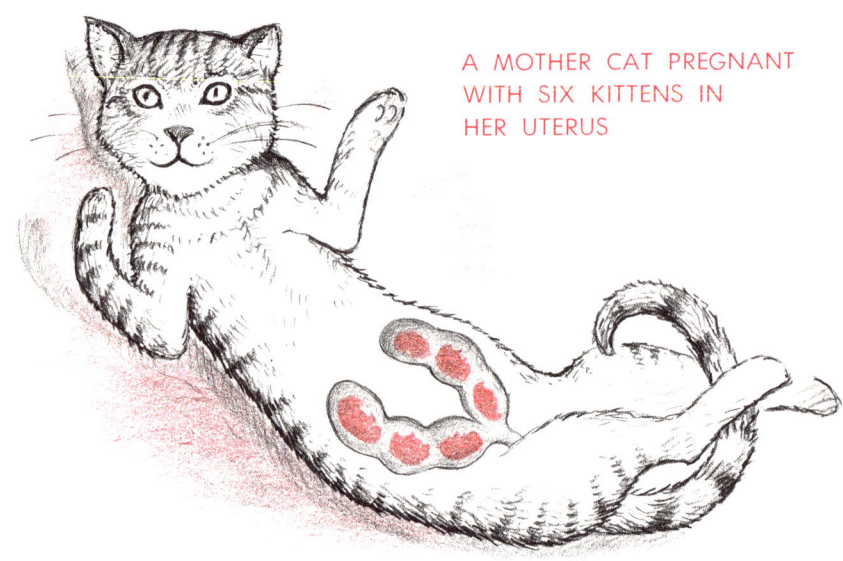
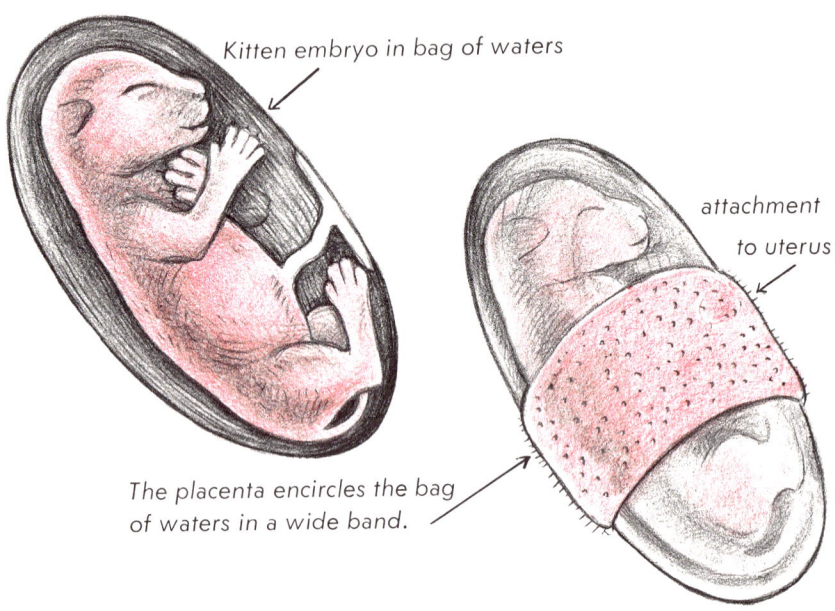

brothers and sisters were developing, the uterus too was growing and the mother cat looked fat.

While the kitten was in the womb it had to have something to grow on—a food supply. This nutrition came from the mother to each kitten through a lifeline—a thin, white cord from the *placenta* to the kitten's navel, or "belly button," or *umbilicus*. The placenta looked something like a circular band attached to the inside of the mother's womb. Blood vessels carrying blood with food dissolved in it run through the placenta, and it is this nutrition that flowed through the cord to the kitten. Each kitten has its own placenta.

When the kittens were ready to be born, the bag of waters broke and a little fluid trickled out of the mother. The womb was made of strong muscle which squeezed down many times, or contracted, to push the kittens down the birth-canal and out. The mother bit the cord in two, and licked away the bag that was still over each kitten, and they began breathing. The placenta, sometimes called the after-birth, came out. The mother usually eats this as she tidies up the nest and takes gentle care of her kittens. She later nurses them with her milk and teaches them as they grow.

The human embryo grows in fairly much the same way, except that there is most often only one in the mother's uterus. The ovum also started out as a tiny cell in one ovary (each mother had two ovaries), and came down a tube, where it was fertilized by a sperm from the father, and on into the uterus. The embryo grew in its own bag of waters, and was nourished through a cord from the placenta, round and flat as a mud pie, attached to the inside of the womb. This embryo also looked a little like a fish at first, and then for a while it looked like the kitten had looked at this stage, or any other mammal embryo, in fact. It is very difficult, or impossible, to tell any early mammal embryos apart as they begin to form.

By the end of the second month, the embryo's growth is well under way, and the little being is slightly over an inch long. It has a new name now, and is called a *fetus* (*feet*-us). Tiny, stubby fingers are visible (but no toes yet). Eyelids, nose, and ears begin to show, though the face itself does not look much like one. As a little embryo it actually had a sort of tail, but as the body grew the tail disappeared, and the fetus began to take on the look of a human form. At the end of three months the fetus is more than twice as long as at two months—approximately two and a half inches. At around four to five and a half months, its mother feels it begin to move, now and then.

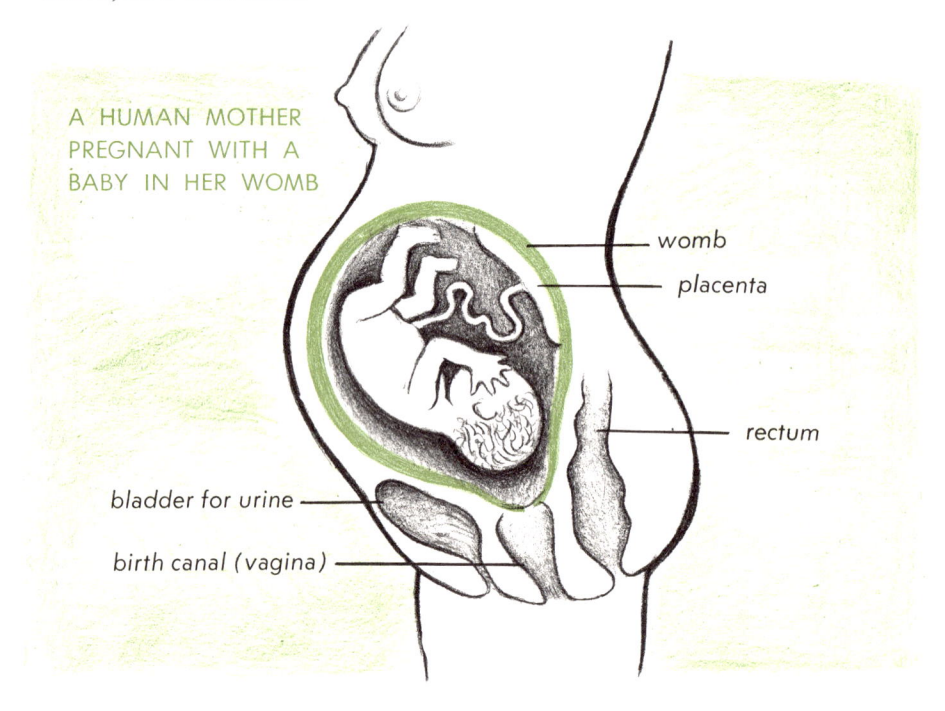

A HUMAN MOTHER PREGNANT WITH A BABY IN HER WOMB

- womb
- placenta
- rectum
- bladder for urine
- birth canal (vagina)

After about nine months the fetus is a baby, ready to be born. The mother's uterus begins to contract every few minutes. At first the contractions are quite far apart. Closer and closer together come these contractions, or labor pains. They are called that because it is real work, or labor, for the mother to give birth to the baby. The bag of waters breaks and some fluid trickles out. The passage slowly widens, and the baby comes down the birth-canal,

Human placenta (cut)

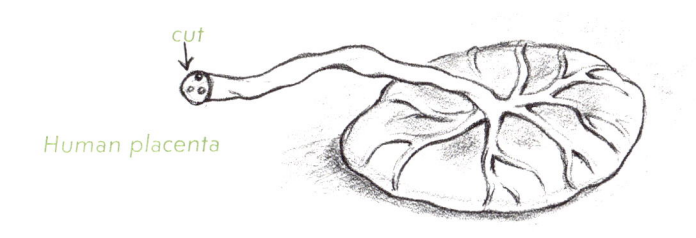

or vagina (va-*jie*-na), into the light of day—probably headfirst (though not all babies come headfirst). Sometimes babies are born at home, but more often in our country nowadays they are born in a hospital. The doctor firmly gets hold of the wet, slippery baby and pats or "spanks" it a few times to help it get started breathing, and then he cuts the cord with scissors. A little bit of cord is left on the baby's navel, but in a few days it will dry up and fall off. The afterbirth, or placenta, comes out and the mother's womb squeezes down, and will eventually become small again. Though this is hard work for the mother, cat or human, she is happy that she is bringing new life into the world.

Back to the egg-layers, and let's take a look at some bird eggs, warm in the parents' nest. The bird embryos had no food supply directly from the mother, no lifeline or umbilical cord. All their nutrition had to be right there in the egg with them, and each little bird could grow on only as much food as the egg could hold.

The egg way was the method by which most creatures reproduced for millions of years of earth's history. Almost all creatures of the sea laid eggs (fishes, lobsters, octopuses, snails), as did insects and spiders, frogs and toad, turtles and lizards, snakes and birds. Land mothers deposited their eggs, as they do today, where they would be safely concealed, for an egg makes a tasty meal to a hungry searcher. Most mothers provided for their babies (and still do) by placing the eggs where they would hatch to find the kind of food they required nearby. Birds take the best care of their fledglings until they are able to go out on their own. But there are limits to what can be done with an egg.

Now we come to the other half of that remarkable double-happening in the story of life.

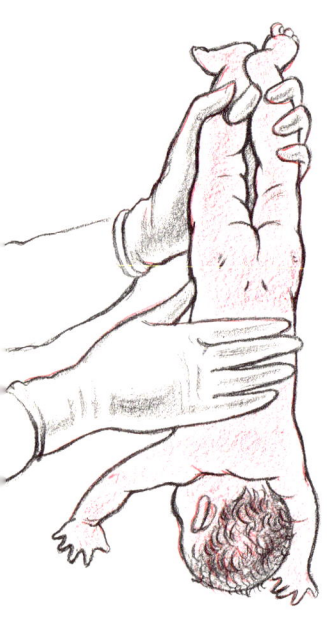

Back to plants. We saw that a new kind of spore in Spore Forest times was somehow held on some unknown tree (or smaller plant) once, instead of blowing forth to become a little gametophyte that grew the new tree from it. This spore held the female sex cell, the egg, inside it, to be fertilized by a sperm which found its way to it. By staying on the parent plant, the little embryo received protection, nutrition, and growing time.

Very much the same thing happened to animals. For, strangely, around the same time (perhaps 100 million years ago), some kind of animal egg, instead of being laid on or in the ground, somehow was held *inside the body* of an unknown animal mother. Here three things could now happen: the embryo could receive protection, nutrition, and growing time. No longer restricted to eggs, a whole vast new wealth of animal life was free to evolve—the world of mammals.

AN IMPORTANT HAPPENING

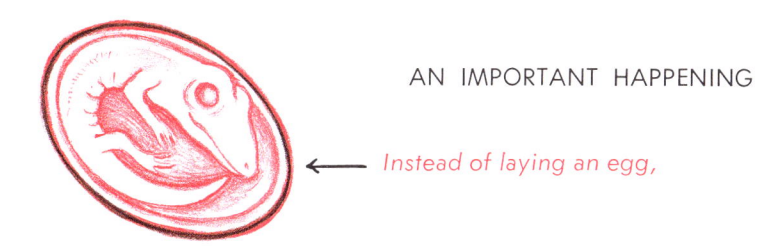

← Instead of laying an egg,

some animal mother of long ago was able to hold the embryo inside her while it developed. →

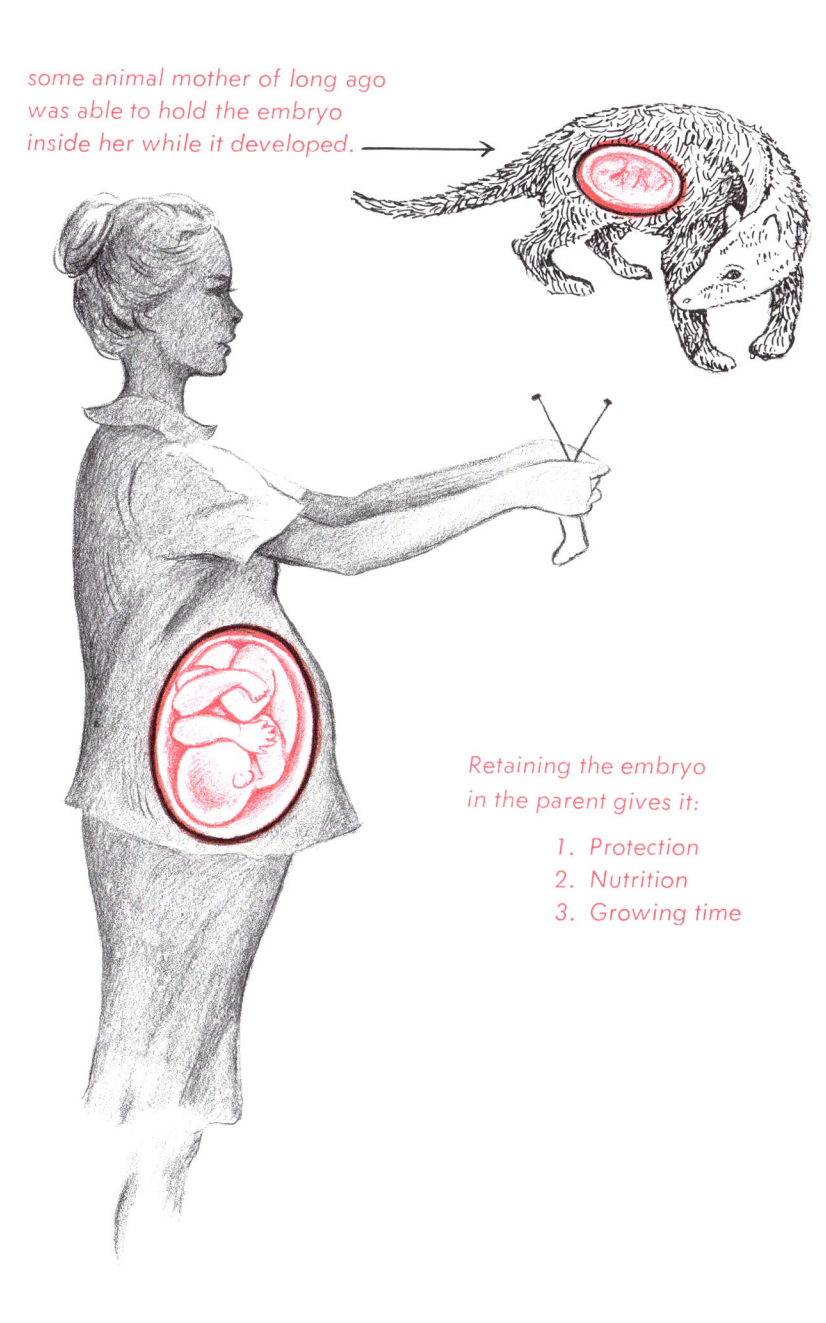

Retaining the embryo in the parent gives it:

1. Protection
2. Nutrition
3. Growing time

When the shell was no longer necessary for outdoor protection in mammals, it became no longer formed in the mother. (A few egg-laying types of animals, such as some snakes, today give birth to live offspring, but this is because the egg remains inside the mother, where the animal hatches. The shell itself is usually reduced to a thin membrane. This is not the same as mammal live births because the little animal did not receive food from its mother through a placenta and cord.) Instead of the few days or weeks that frogs, turtles, and birds could develop in their eggs on a limited food supply, mammals could take months in the mother—could even take around a year (horses) or about two years (elephants). No egg could ever be big enough to pack that much food supply in it and still be safely hidden. Mammals, in growing a longer time, could develop longer legs and bigger brains. They could travel farther, think better.

The placenta of the calf fetus attaches to the mother cow in patches.

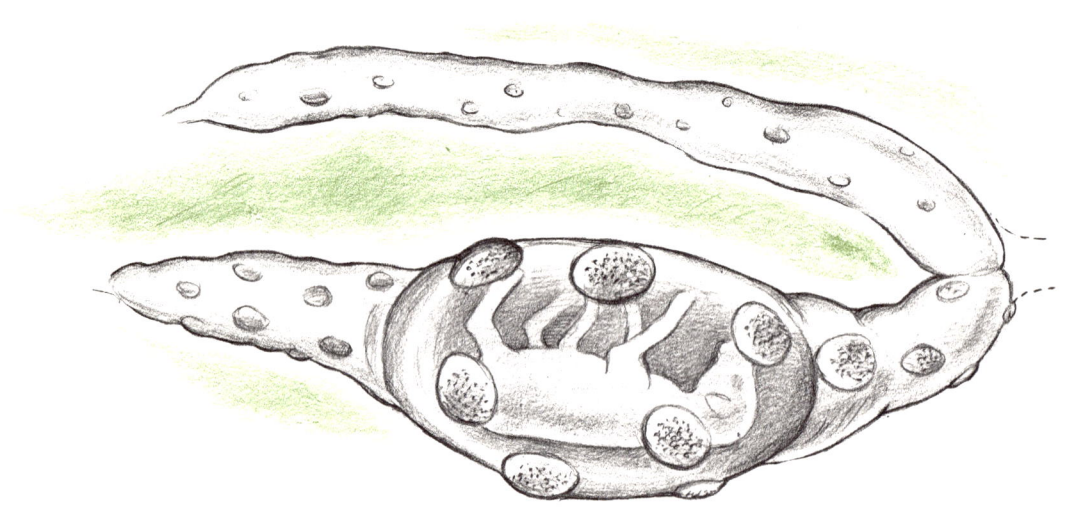

7. The Father

By now you are probably wondering how the egg became fertilized inside the mother.

We saw how, in seed-forming plants, one plant gave something to another that fertilized the ovule. This joining together is a basic idea behind the sex system in all living things. In plant or animal, the special cell which carries the material by traveling can be called the male sex cell; the one that "stays put" is the female sex cell. Because the male cell is smaller it travels more easily; because the female cell stores food (a little or much) it is almost always larger, and therefore less able to travel. The small traveler must have a means of movement, and throughout the animal kingdom, almost all male sex cells, or sperms, have "tails" that lash them forward. Many plant sperms also are moved by tail-like flagella, though others move in ways not clearly understood.

Sperms, then, of plants and animals are remarkably similar in three ways. First, they move or swim in some manner. Second, they always come in huge numbers, usually millions at a time from one male individual. In the spring the powderlike pollen from many trees and flowers, bearing uncountable numbers of sperms, may cover leaves and grass with golden-yellow dust. Only if there are many are a few likely to find the female cell in enormous space. In a male mammal, there are always millions of sperms that travel together at a time. When they enter the female they must travel a long distance for their size. It is as if a female sex cell, or ovum, were a marble at the other end of a gym floor and someone tried to hit it by rolling a handful of small beads at it. Third, the sperms must always be in a liquid, or otherwise they would both dry out and be unable to swim or travel. (The pollen grain, though in air, carries a sperm inside it, and goes into action in the moisture of the pistil.)

In certain animals, such as the octopus and squid, the sperms are in packets of a substance like gelatin, which one special arm of the male places under a hoodlike fold of the female's skin, where it softens and the sperms move on their way into her body. In mammals the sperms are in a fluid; sperms and fluid together are called *semen* (*sea*-men).

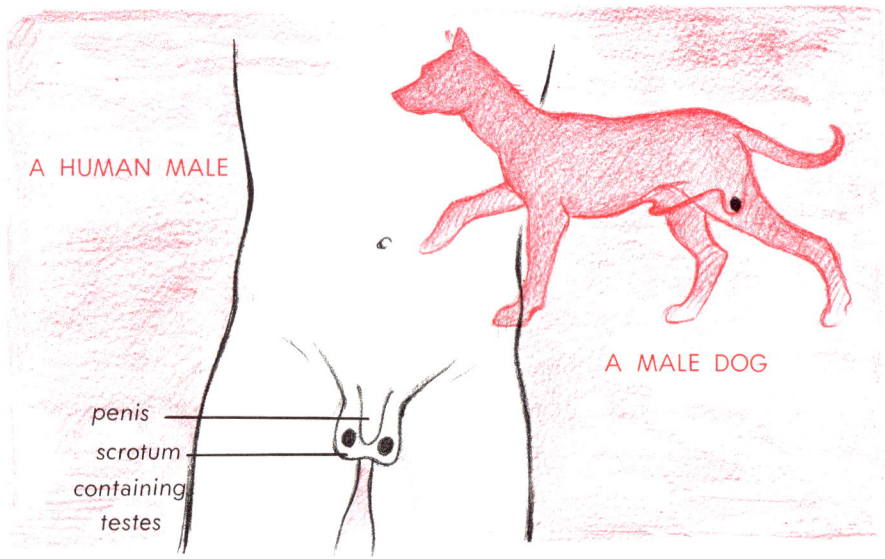

A HUMAN MALE

A MALE DOG

penis
scrotum
containing
testes

Sperms are made in two organs in the male, small and ball-like, called testes. (One is a testis. They are also sometimes called *testicles*.) In man and most mammals these are in a bag of skin, the scrotum (*scroe-tum*), which hangs between the legs, somewhat outside the body. The sperms leave the body through the penis (*pea-nis*). This contains a long tube, through which a water solution, the urine, leaves the body when he goes to the bathroom. (In females, urine comes out a different opening than the vagina.) Urine and

frog sperm　*chicken sperm*　*sheep sperm*　*snail sperm*

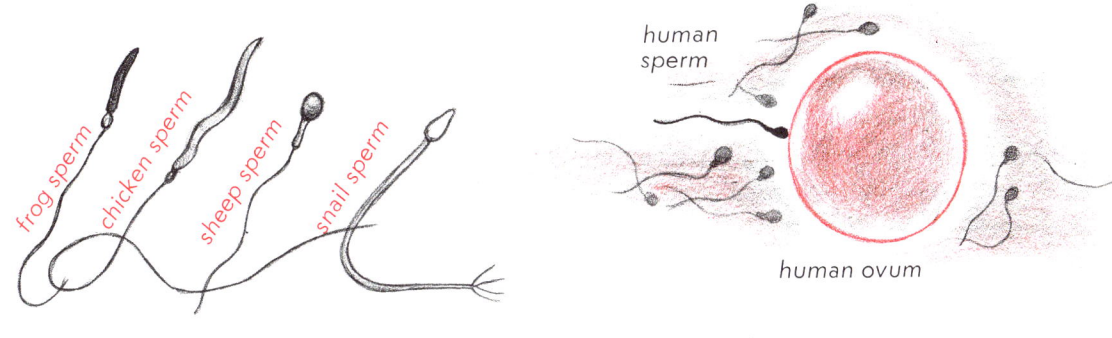

human sperm

human ovum

semen never come out at the same time. When the male places his penis in the vagina of the female, the sperms, swimming in the semen, are sent on their journey toward the ovum. In some kinds of animals the male and female select each other with great care and remain mates for life. In human beings this is an act of love and the mates choose each other well, because this is the only way an embryo can be assured of being born and growing up as a person with a father and mother who love and want it, and will take good care of it.

In the case of most fishes, the male swims around and around, or near, the female, and they release their sperms and eggs into the water at about the same time, where they unite. Eggs of lakes, rivers, and sea are clear and lack hard coverings. But in land eggs, how is the little sperm ever to penetrate the hard shell? In a bean, the very small hole through which the pollen tube reached the egg can be seen. But have you ever seen such an opening in a hen's egg? The answer is that the sperm got in before there was a shell. For there is more to an egg than just the egg. The egg itself, or more correctly the ovum, is the round, yellow sphere you can examine in a hen's egg, and almost all of this is food supply, or yolk. The embryo would have begun forming in a little pale circle you may find on the yolk. The hen's egg you eat has almost certainly not met a sperm and been fertilized. Hens can lay eggs which have not been fertilized; wild birds cannot. As the big, yellow ovum comes down the mother's long, twisting egg tube, the egg white is added from glands along the way, and last of all the shell. The sperm has a long way to travel up the egg tube to meet the ovum before the rest is added.

We learned that all parts are present, however small, in a baby before birth. In a newborn boy the testes are there, and in a girl baby the ovaries are present. These remain quiet and dormant during childhood. That is a time when boys and girls are curious about the world and are busy discovering all kinds of things about it and how to live in it. When the boy and girl become "teen-agers" their bodies begin to achieve full development. Teen-agers are also called *adolescents*, which means "becoming adult." During this time they are getting to know themselves and each other better, so that when they are fully grown and ready to take their places in the world they will be able to make the best choice of a mate.

8. Why?

Having learned something about the way the two-parent method works in plants and animals, we are left with a question: why is there a two-sex system? But first we need to examine other systems, and then ask: why does the two-sex system work better than other ways—or does it?

The plant world has many forms of reproduction, as we saw in Chapter 4. There was fission, the split-in-two way; there was the break-into-many fragments method; there were zoospores that burst out of algae cells and swam away; and dry spores that were produced and blew away.

You can carry out some interesting experiments of your own. Try putting a potato in water, and watch it grow attractive leaves, stem, and roots. Potatoes sometimes "bud" new little ones on them also. Strawberry and other plants put out runners—long, stringlike stems that grow a whole new little plant on each tip, and lilies-of-the-valley send out root runners all over the place, from which new leaves and flowers spring up. You can find an onion even sprouting in the refrigerator, or an underground tulip or daffodil bulb that has multiplied into a whole cluster of bulbs. Pussy willows in a vase may put out roots, and for centuries farmers and gardeners have made living fences by sticking branches (such as from a willow tree) into moist soil and letting them take root and burst into leaf. Common house plants, such as geranium or philodendron, will grow from a slip—a small branch put into moist soil or water, and an African violet may grow a new plant from practically every leaf, if you are lucky and skillful at raising them this way. How much easier to grow new plants these ways than to wait for flowers, and let them go through the whole, long, complicated process of fertilization and seed-making!

And then we may well look into the animal world. *Euglena*, the little plant-animal, reproduced by fission, and many small, single-celled animal species that may be watched under the microscope also split in two. One of these is *Paramecium*. This common little creature zips about under the lens looking like a boat with hundreds of short oars, and if you watch some long enough, you are likely to see one going through the process of dividing. (Note that *Paramecium* divides across, while *Euglena* divides the long way.)

Then there is *Daphnia*, the water flea. It is really not a flea (which is an insect) at all, but more closely related to crabs and shrimps, even though it is just the size of a speck. You can sometimes find a pool or pond alive with them, or an aquarium store or pet shop that sells live fish may have some. They are fascinating to study because they are practically transparent.

Daphnia is really amazing because all spring, summer, and into early fall each female, although there are no males to fertilize it, produces uncountable numbers of offspring, and all of them are daughters. Of course great mouthfuls are devoured by fish and other hungry water-dwellers.

You can search a meadow, field, or garden (particularly on the roses) and usually find aphids—tiny insects that sometimes heavily coat stems, tender leaves, and flower buds. They come in several colors, even bright red or green. These aphid females can go through spring and summer also producing thousands of young, with no male to play his part, and like *Daphnia*, all the offspring are females. There are other insects also that reproduce by this strange procedure.

Still another kind of reproduction in some animals is *budding*. The interesting jellyfish—not really a fish at all, or anything like one

—could hardly be expected to do anything the way anything else does it. Jellyfishes bud new little jellyfishes off themselves. These are perfectly formed, miniature ones that grow on various parts of the parent, and while still small, break loose and swim away. Many jellyfishes also produce an entirely different form of themselves, called a *polyp*, which goes off to attach itself to the sea bottom or an underwater stone or log. This little flowerlike polyp, that waves its "arms" to catch food, buds more tiny polyps off itself, but it also buds off little jellyfishes that go floating off to become larger and larger.

What of the starfish, also not truly a fish at all? It has still another way of making new replicas of itself, for many kinds split in two along lines through the center. One kind, found in the Pacific Ocean, has arms that break off. Each half, or each arm of the latter kind, grows into a whole new starfish. Fishermen know what pests starfish can be, for when they are cut apart, each arm will grow a complete new animal, so long as a little of the central portion remains attached to the arm.

There are many worm types in the world, a great many that live in the sea, some flowery or feathery and of beautiful colors, and scarcely looking like worms at all. It is quite common for worms to break into fragments, or grow parts that break off and develop into new worms. Some break into many sections that remain attached, like a chain, and when this becomes fairly long, some segments of it will free themselves to go off and form new worms. Others simply

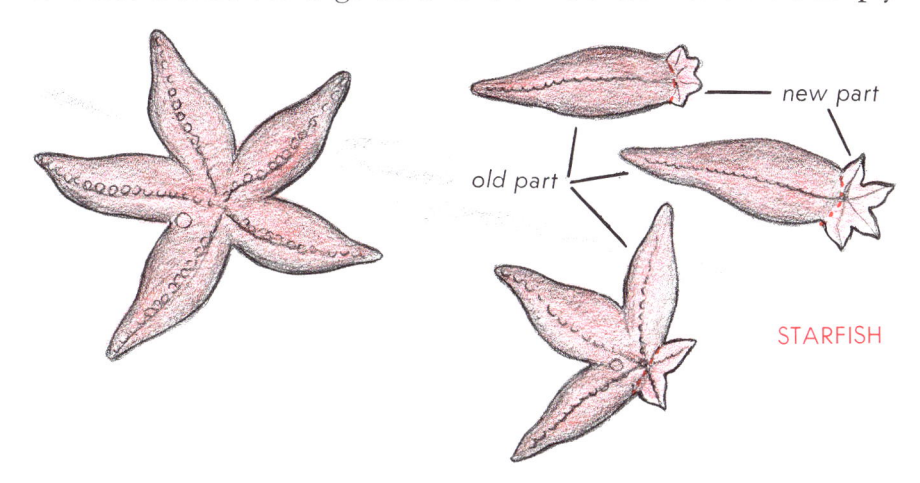

STARFISH

PARAMECIUM

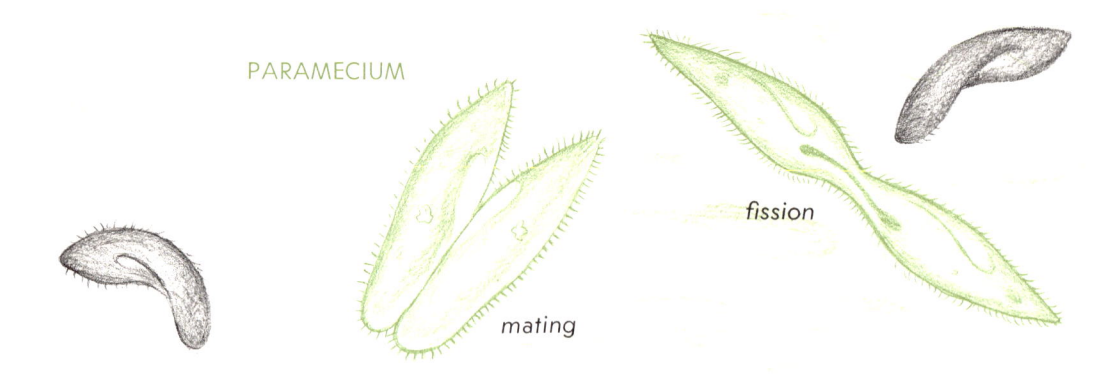

mating

fission

break in half, crosswise. When the common earthworm is cut in two, the head end will grow into a new earthworm.

There are eggs of certain animals (for example, the rabbit) that have been made, in experiments, to develop into new animals without being fertilized by a father animal. Why, then, with all these no-sex methods, does there bother to be a two-sex system? There are quicker and easier ways to reproduce, and all these ways seem to work very well. But why does not a cow or cat or human being simply break off a leg that grows into a new calf, kitten, or child? Why does not a mammal bud off a new one of itself, or break up into parts, and each part grow whole again, somewhat the way broken bones and wounded skin heals? Why cannot females simply produce new females that will produce new females? Is the male of any use at all in reproduction?

If we take a longer look at the *Paramecium*, watching through the microscope until our eyes grow weary, putting a new drop of water on the glass slide as the old begins to dry away, we may come suddenly upon a surprising sight. For we may see two *Parameciums* come together and seem to stick, side by side, continuing to swim about this way. Later they part, and still later each divides into four new *Parameciums*.

There was an exchange of material between them. Each one gave something to the other. The two looked exactly alike. They could not be said to be male and female; the meeting looked like

DAPHNIA

eggs

just any encounter between *Parameciums*. Yet the two were of different types, for not just any two can come together.

The surprise event occurs in *Daphnia*, too. Through spring and summer and into the fall she rapidly produces daughters all over the pond, but later in fall—behold, she has given birth to some males, which mate with the females. Again the male gives something to the female, and eggs begin developing. Each egg has a tough case, and winters over through cold weather and into the next spring, when it hatches into a female. This happens also when food shortage threatens, or drought, or other difficult living conditions. Male aphids, too, appear to fertilize the females.

Something similar occurs in the lives of jellyfish and starfish. Each busily buds or breaks into pieces to reproduce through sunny, warm months, but "rest" through the coldest winter weather. Early spring comes along and the seas are suddenly full of male and female jellyfish producing young. The starfish arms almost bulge with great quantities of eggs let loose into the water to meet with thousands of sperms, and through the union of eggs and sperms, millions of tiny dancing specks are formed that go floating off

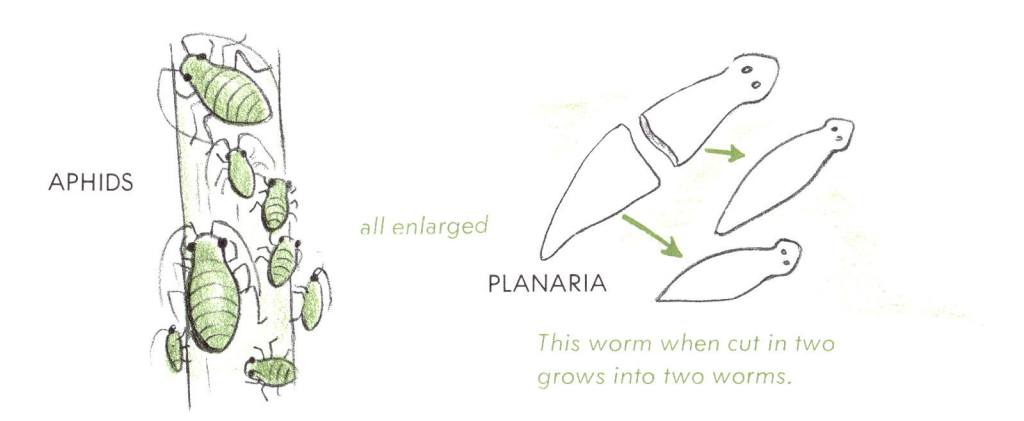

APHIDS

all enlarged

PLANARIA

This worm when cut in two grows into two worms.

Jellyfish budding

through the sparkling waters until settling down to grow into new starfish.

If we put these facts together and study them, what do we notice? We notice three things.

First, the simpler methods without a male (fission, budding, breaking into fragments) produce the largest numbers in the easiest ways.

Second, that in all these cases (except *Euglena*), now and then the two-parent sex system comes along. In fact, it has been found in experiments that *Parameciums* die out after a while if the exchange of material between different specimens is prevented, and this holds true for some other animals and plants, also.

Third, that most of these animal forms we have observed start out the spring with young that have been made by the two-sex

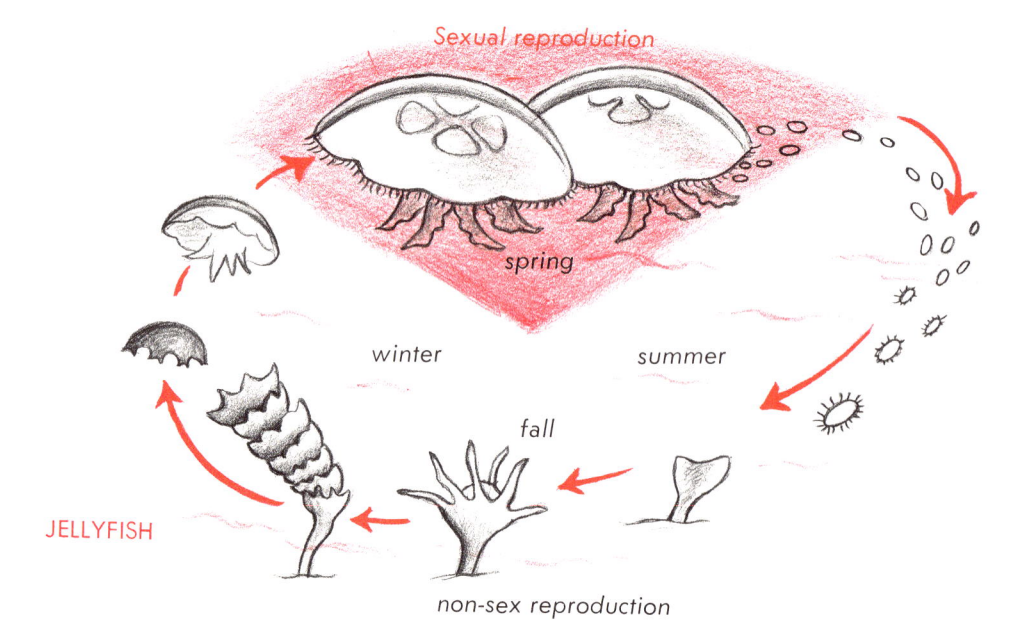

Sexual reproduction

spring

winter

summer

fall

JELLYFISH

non-sex reproduction

method. Either they made tough little eggs, as *Daphnia* did, just before the cold weather or hard times set in, or made males and females in the fall, as the jellyfish did, that mated the next spring.

We can conclude from these three facts that maybe the sex method is not useful so much for producing large numbers as for something else. Mammals never produce thousands of young at a time, or even in a year. A field mouse may have as many as a hundred baby mice a year, and some rabbits may have three or four litters totalling twenty or so young rabbits from one spring to the next, but such mammals as deer and horses usually produce only one or two offspring in a year, and lions and tigers seldom more than three or four. The mixing-together of two sex cells, then, the giving of a little material from one to another, seems to do something else. It seems to bring a new strength into life. Animals as well as plants coming from only one parent, instead of by means of the sex system, are almost always exactly like that parent. But with the male-and-female way, each brings something separate to the union.

Whom do you look most like, your mother or your father? You may have your mother's red hair and your father's blue eyes. These are *traits* which you inherited. Every tiny bit of you, each cell in "knowing" how to grow, has inherited something from your parents and grandparents all the way back to the start of life on earth. Sexual reproduction, then, causes new types of living things by the combining of assorted traits, some from this ancestor, some from that. But you are still yourself, an individual like no one else on earth (unless you have an identical twin, in which case you have inherited the same traits).

What is this material passed from the sperm to the egg, and how does it work? The answers are not completely understood at present. In every single plant and animal cell are threadlike *chromosomes,* so very small that many aspects of them cannot even be studied with the strongest microscope, so that many other methods must be used. The unfertilized egg possesses the same number of chromosomes as the sperm, and at the time of fertilization, when the two cells combine into one, it is these chromosomes contributed by both father and mother that determine the manner of growth of every single cell that will be in the body of the embryo. It is through these that the child inherits certain traits from one parent, other traits from the other parent. He will grow up to pass on some of them in his time to his children, as his ancestors passed them down from far back in time.

Nothing much was known about chromosomes until this century, and there is much yet to be discovered. This whole, vast subject is the study of *genetics*, in which scientists think and experiment to learn more about the inheritance of traits, the secrets of the cell, and something of the riddle of life.

Let us suppose that the woods are full of brown rabbits that melt

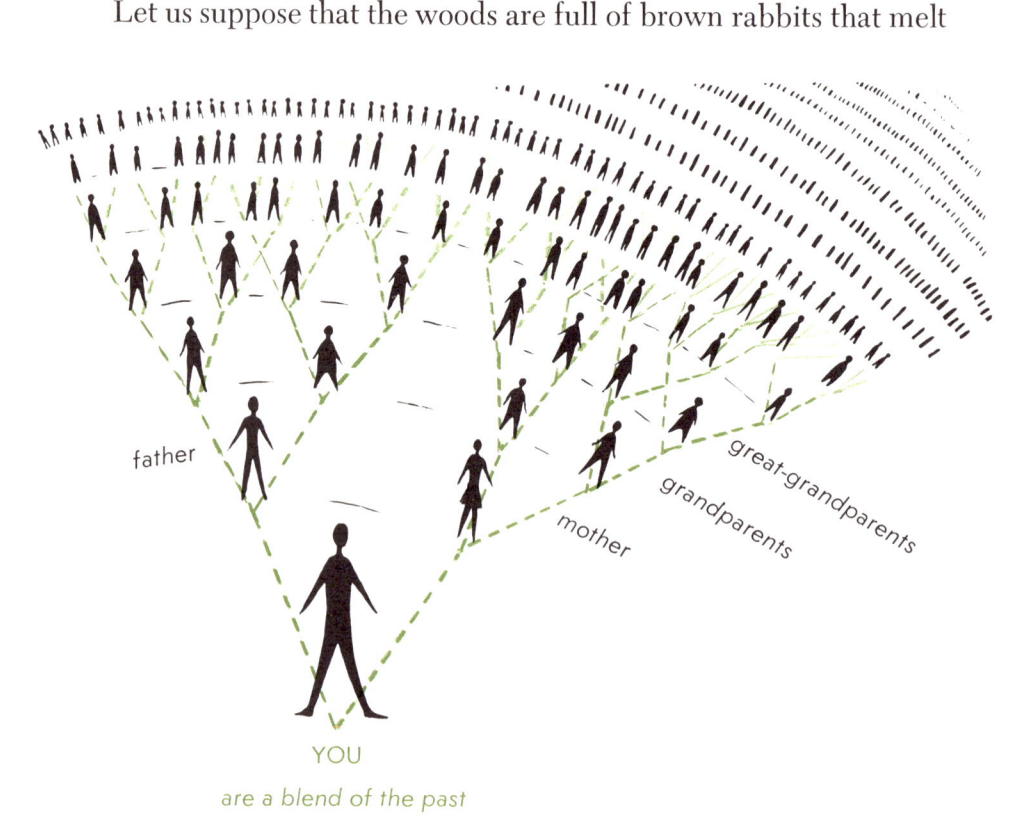

YOU
are a blend of the past

GREGOR MENDEL

into the shadows, able to hide from searching eyes. If a white rabbit happens to be born it will stand out as if in a spotlight, and won't live long enough, probably, to have children of its own. But suppose an unusually snowy winter comes along. It is the brown rabbit, standing out like a silhouette against fresh-fallen snow, that will be snapped up by a hungry fox or owl, while its white brother will be practically invisible. If the white should mate with a brown and there should be little ones of both colors, it is the white ones that will be most likely to survive—while there is snow. And so the mixing-together of chromosomes brings *change* into the world that helps life meet new conditions.

Before anyone knew there were any such things as chromosomes, very few people ever wondered why elephant babies look like elephant parents, instead of something else, and why mice newborn grow up to look like their mice parents, cell for cell. But some few people in the past have wondered how this came about. One was a monk, Gregor Mendel, who, a century ago, in a life full of struggle and disappointment, carried out some of the first and most important, truly scientific, experiments ever done. This was in what was Austria at that time, now a part of Czechoslovakia.

What Mendel did was this: in the garden of the monastery he planted purebred pea plants (meaning that their parents had been

A LAW THAT MENDEL DISCOVERED

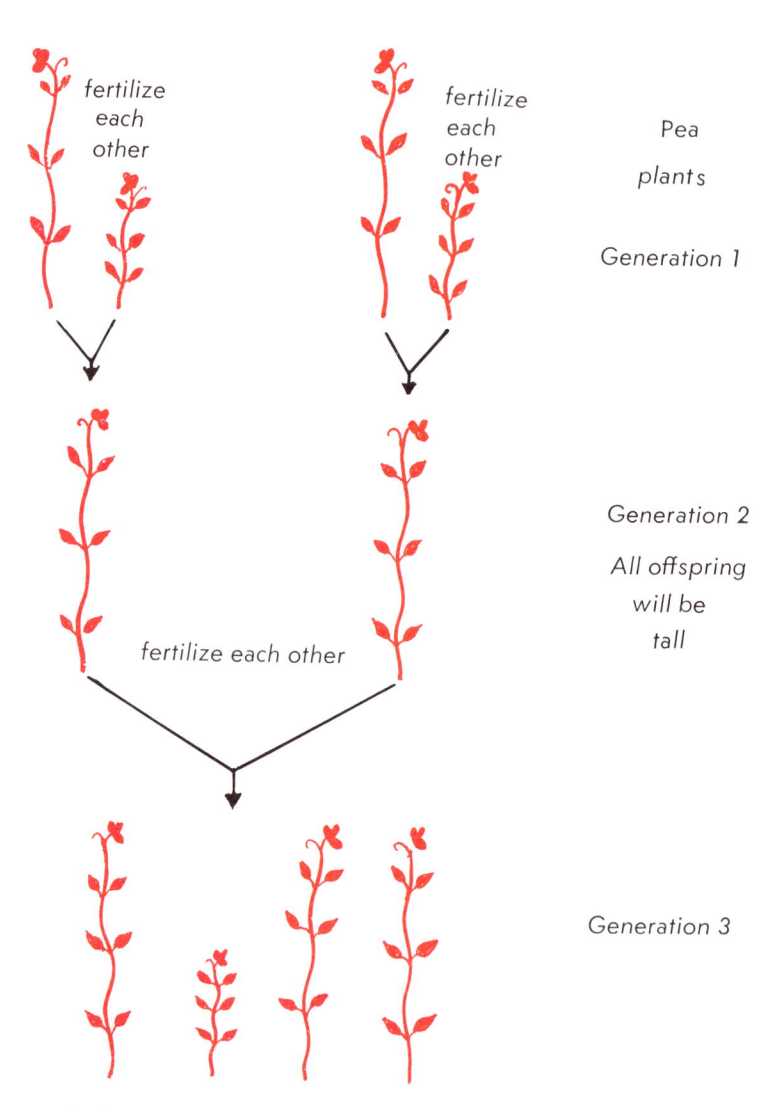

fertilize each other

fertilize each other

Pea plants

Generation 1

Generation 2

All offspring will be tall

fertilize each other

Generation 3

In Generation 3, three out of every four offspring will bear the tall or dominant trait; one out of every four will have the short or recessive trait.

MENDEL'S LAW IN GUINEA PIGS

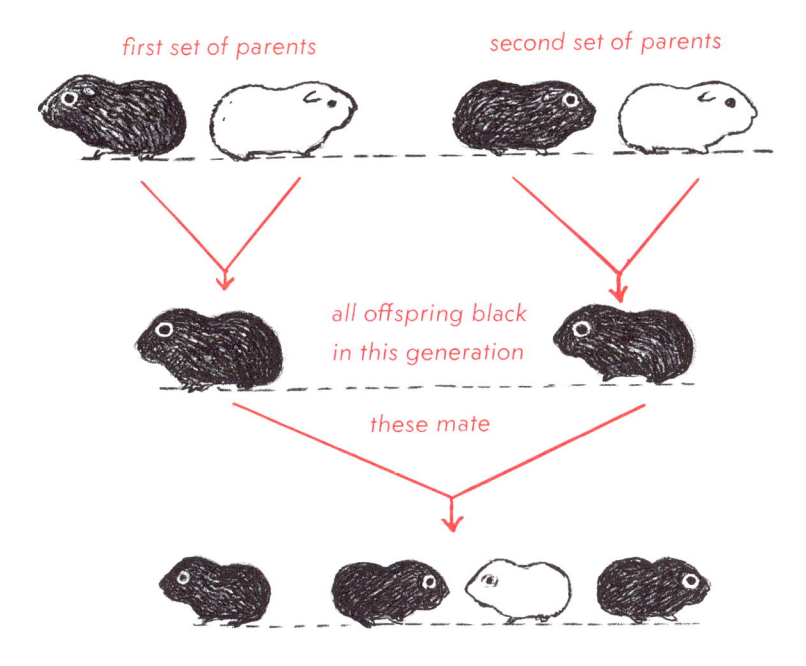

first set of parents *second set of parents*

all offspring black in this generation

these mate

*Three have black or dominant trait.
One has white or recessive trait.*

The tiny fruit fly (Drosophila) is used frequently for experiments because it breeds quickly, can be raised in glass jars, and has some large chromosomes.

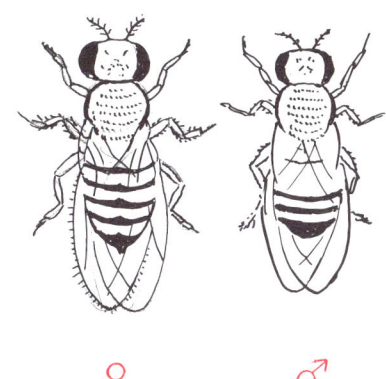

♀   ♂

of exactly the same type for many generations back). Some were of a tall variety, some dwarf. He allowed these to fertilize each other, because he was curious to determine how many of their seeds would produce tall plants and how many would produce dwarf ones. Later he also crossed pure plants bearing green peas with some bearing yellow ones, and having other traits. His startling discoveries laid the groundwork for the whole science of genetics. Mendel did not know at this time about chromosomes; no one knew for sure how the body passed on its inheritance of traits, and so his work is all the more remarkable. His life makes good reading, and though his findings were not appreciated in his lifetime, his memory will live long.

Almost every kind of plant and animal uses the two-sex system at least once in a while (a few never seem to) as its manner of reproducing. The uniting, the mixing-together, the inheritance of different traits, has brought new directions to the forms of life on earth. It is through having new kinds of living things that there have come some able to face new hardships and challenges. The non-sex, the one-parent ways brought quantity; the idea of the sex way, the two-parent system—the family plan—brings fewer and better kinds.

Change has brought hundreds of thousands of types of plants that go forth in dozens of ways on their journeys before they germinate, able to live in the hottest and coldest, wettest and driest, regions of the world. Animals swim or fly, run or crawl, *after* they hatch or are born and do some growing, enough to go forth and find new space to stretch and breathe and seek a living.

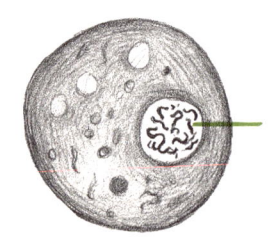

Chromosomes visible in cell nucleus.

WHY

IS THE SEX SYSTEM SO WIDESPREAD WHEN OTHER METHODS OF REPRODUCTION CAN PRODUCE LARGER NUMBERS OF OFFSPRING MORE SIMPLY?

The human being is prepared for the best start-off of all. It not only develops a long time inside the mother, but it goes through the longest growing-up period after it is born of any animal, with two parents to help it until it is mature. Being mature means achieving fullest development of mind as well as body that it can —finding happiness by doing the best it can with what it has to work with.

Human beings can do their "traveling," not by flying or running or swimming away, so much as by becoming mature. They then are able to choose their mate well, because thoughtfully producing and raising offspring, and making a good family, is the best use of sex and the two-parent system.

BECAUSE

THE SEX SYSTEM RESULTS IN COMBINING OF TRAITS FROM BOTH THE PARENTS, CAUSES NEW INDIVIDUALS THAT CAN MEET NEW CONDITIONS. IT CAUSES CHANGE.

INHERITING THE BEST OF THE OLD BUILDS NEW STRENGTHS.

Index

acorn, 13
after-ripening, 14
afterbirth, 35, 37
algae, 22, 23, 25
anther, 17, 18
aphids, 46, 49
apple, 14

bag of waters, 33, 34, 35
bananas, 8
beans, 8, 11, 12, 13, 18, 19
bear, 33
birth canal, 36
budding, 45, 46, 50

capsule, 9, 10
cat, 33, 34, 38
cell, 56
cell, egg, 33
    female sex, 19, 41
    male sex, 19, 41
chimpanzee, 33, 40, 48
chromosomes, 51, 52, 55, 56
cotyledons, 13

Daphnia, 46, 49, 51
date palm, 13, 14
dicot, 13, 14
dog, 33, 42
dormancy, 14
Drosophila, 55
drupe, 19

earthworm, 48
egg, bird's, 31, 37, 40
    fish, 43
    hen's, 31, 43
    insect, 31, 37
    of the sea, 37, 43
    plant, 18, 19
    reptile, 31, 37, 39, 40
embryo, 11, 19, 26, 31-40, 43
Euglena, 21, 22, 30, 32, 46, 50

female, 19
female sex cell, 41
fertilization, 18, 19, 41, 42, 52
fetus, 35, 36
fishes, 37, 43
fission, 21, 22, 23
flagella, 25, 41
forests, ancient, 25, 29
fragmenting, 23, 30
fruit fly, 55

gametophyte, 26, 29
generations, alternating, 26
genetics, 52
germination, 13, 14
grapefruit, 14
guinea pigs, 55

hay fever, 16

insects, 19, 20, 28, 29

jellyfish, 46, 47, 49, 50, 51

kitten, 11, 33-35

labor pains, 36, 37
lions, 33, 52
lotus, 16

male sex cell, 19, 41
mammals, 32, 33, 38, 40, 41, 51
maple tree, 9, 10
Mendel, Gregor, 53-56
mice, 33, 38, 51
micropyle, 18, 19
monocot, 13, 14
moss, 28

navel, 35, 37
nectaries, 20
nursing, 32, 35

octopus, 42
orange, 13, 14
ovary, 18, 30, 33, 35, 44
ovule, 19, 41
ovum, 33, 41, 43

Paramecium, 46, 48, 49, 50
peas, 53, 54, 56
penis, 42, 43
petals, 17, 18
pistil, 17, 18, 19
placenta, 34, 37, 40
Planaria, 49
pods, 9, 11, 30
pollen, 14, 18, 19, 20, 28, 41, 42
pollination, 18, 19, 20
polyp, 47, 50
Protococcus, 22

rabbit, 48, 51, 52, 53

ragweed, 14
Rockweed, 25

scrotum, 42
seaweed, 24, 25
seed containers, 10, 11, 30
seed leaves, 13
seed pods, 8, 9
seedlings, 16
seeds that cling, 12
seeds with parachutes, 8
seeds with wings, 10
semen, 42
slip, 45
snakes, 40, 45
sperms, 19, 25, 26, 33, 41, 42, 43
Spirogyra, 23
spores, 25, 26, 28, 29, 30, 38
squid, 42
stamens, 17, 30
starfish, 47, 49

testes, 42, 44
testicles, 42, 44
traits, 51, 52, 56

Ulothrix, 23, 24
umbilicus, 35
uterus, 33, 34, 35

vagina, 36, 37, 42, 43

water flea, 46
weeds, 14
willow, 14
womb, 32, 33, 36, 37
worms, 47, 48, 49

zoospores, 23, 25, 30
zygospores, 23, 24, 25, 30
zygote, 25

The Author-Illustrator

MARGARET COSGROVE was born in Sylvania, Ohio, and became interested in botany and biology at an early age. After attending the Art Institute of Chicago and the University of Chicago, Miss Cosgrove came to New York where she spent some years as a medical illustrator in several large hospitals. She has broadened her interests to include all the natural sciences, and has written, as well as illustrated, books in many of these fields. Much of her time has been spent working with children of all ages and backgrounds.